Access Reading

1

Reading in the Real World

Tim Collins
National–Louis University

THOMSON ™

HEINLE

Australia   Canada   Mexico   Singapore   United Kingdom   United States

THOMSON

★ ™

HEINLE

Access Reading 1: Reading in the Real World
Tim Collins

Publisher: *James W. Brown*
Senior Acquisitions Editor: *Sherrise Roehr*
Director of ESL/Global ELT Development: *Anita Raducanu*
Associate Development Editor: *Yeny Kim*
Senior Production Editor: *Lianne Ames*
Director of Marketing: *Amy Mabley*
Senior Marketing Manager: *Donna Lee Kennedy*

Senior Print Buyer: *Mary Beth Hennebury*
Compositor: *Thompson Steele*
Project Manager: *Thompson Steele*
Copyeditor: *Thompson Steele*
Cover Illustrator: *Nip Rogers*
Cover Designer: *Ha Nguyen*
Text Designer: *Sue Gerould*
Printer: *Transcontinental Printing*

For permission to use material from this text or product contact us:

Tel	1-800-730-2214
Fax	1-800-730-2215
Web	www.thomsonrights.com

Library of Congress Cataloging-in-Publication Data

Collins, Tim.
  Access reading : reading in the real world / Tim Collins.
    p. cm.
  Includes bibliographical references and index.
    ISBN 0-8837-7061-X (bk. 1) -- ISBN 0-8837-064-4 (bk. 2)
      1. English language--Textbooks for foreign speakers. 2. Readers.
  I. Title.
PE1128.C6525 2004
428.6'4--dc22

2003061265

Contents

Access Reading 1 Scope and Sequence

Unit and Title	Readings	Reading Strategy	Graphic Organizer	Study Skill
1 Getting Along *page 2*	Read a profile of a school official. Read about making friends in a new place.	Use pictures and the title to find the main idea.	Use listing.	Find a study buddy.
2 Around Town *page 12*	Read a profile of an immigrant family. Read an interview with a firefighter who helps children.	Use the first sentence of each paragraph to find the main idea.	Use a chart to organize information.	Staying organized.
3 Keeping Busy *page 22*	Read a memo at work. Read an appointment book.	Scan for specific dates and times.	Use an appointment book to organize information.	Use an appointment book.
4 Money in Your Pocket *page 32*	Read a brochure about a supermarket customer card. Read a list of restaurant specials.	Read and draw conclusions.	Use a chart to organize information.	Healthful snacks.
5 Taking Care of Yourself *page 42*	Read about staying safe at work. Read about preventing accidental poisonings at home.	Use pictures and captions to find the main idea.	Use a chart to organize numbers.	Taking breaks.

EFF	SCANS	CASAS
Become and stay informed. Form and express ideas and opinions. Work together. Promote family growth and development.	Understand social systems. Work well with people. Acquire and evaluate data. Interpret and communicate information.	Communicate in interpersonal interactions. Communicate personal information.
Become and stay informed. Form and express ideas and opinions. Work together. Promote family growth and development. Strengthen the family system. Do the work. Work with others.	Teach others. Work well with people. Understand social systems. Acquire and evaluate data. Interpret and communicate information. Serve customers.	Communicate in interpersonal interactions. Communicate personal information. Use the telephone and telephone book. Use community services. Understand basic safety procedures. Use community services to achieve community integration.
Become and stay informed. Form and express ideas and opinions. Meet family needs and responsibilities. Do the work. Work with others. Work within the big picture.	Allocate time and money. Understand organizational systems. Monitor and correct performance. Acquire and evaluate data. Interpret and communicate information.	Communicate in interpersonal interactions. Communicate personal information. Understand concepts related to job performance. Communicate effectively in the workplace. Identify effective time management skills.
Become and stay informed. Form and express ideas and opinions. Meet family needs and responsibilities. Do the work. Work with others. Work within the big picture.	Allocate money and materials. Understand organizational systems. Serve customers. Acquire and evaluate data. Interpret and communicate information.	Communicate in interpersonal interactions. Communicate personal information. Apply principles of comparison shopping. Understand methods used to make purchases. Understand wages. Communicate effectively at work.
Become and stay informed. Form and express ideas and opinions. Meet family needs and responsibilities. Do the work. Work within the big picture.	Monitor and correct performance. Understand organizational systems. Acquire and evaluate data. Interpret and communicate information. Apply technology to specific tasks.	Communicate in interpersonal interactions. Communicate personal information. Understand basic safety procedures. Understand work-related safety standards and procedures. Use the telephone.

Access Reading 1   Scope and Sequence

Unit and Title	Readings	Reading Strategy	Graphic Organizer	Study Skill
6 Tools and Technology *page 52*	Read an ad about new phone features (caller ID, etc.). Read instructions for a machine at work.	Use background information to help you read.	Use a KWL chart to help you read.	Use a computer.
7 Our History *page 62*	Read an article about mural art. Read an article about famous immigrants.	Use related words to help you read.	Use a Venn diagram to organize information.	Use an encyclopedia.
8 Home Sweet Home *page 72*	Read a brochure for an apartment complex. Read a community profile.	Scan for specific information.	Use a T-chart to organize information.	Create a study place.
9 Fun and Relaxation *page 82*	Read a sports center ad. Read about lowering stress.	Use the context to figure out new words.	Use a chart to compare information.	Figuring out new words.
10 Lifelong Learning *page 92*	Read about how to send an e-mail. Read about an adult learning center that receives an award.	Read and make inferences.	Use charts to organize information.	Getting access to a computer.

EFF	SCANS	CASAS
Become and stay informed. Form and express ideas and opinions. Meet family needs and responsibilities. Do the work. Work within the big picture.	Allocate money and materials. Acquire and evaluate data. Interpret and communicate information. Understand technological systems. Select equipment. Apply technology to specific tasks.	Communicate in interpersonal interactions. Communicate personal information. Understand procedures for the use of personal possessions. Effectively use common workplace technology. Communicate effectively in the workplace. Understand how technological systems work.
Become and stay informed. Form and express ideas and opinions. Work together. Take action to strengthen communities. Strengthen the family system.	Teach others. Work well with people of diverse backgrounds. Acquire and evaluate information. Interpret and communicate information. Understand social systems.	Communicate in interpersonal interactions. Communicate personal information. Understand aspects of society and culture. Understand historical information. Understand effective personal management.
Become and stay informed. Form and express ideas and opinions. Work together. Meet family needs and responsibilities.	Allocate space. Acquire and evaluate data. Interpret and communicate information. Understand social systems.	Communicate in interpersonal interactions. Communicate personal information. Understand concepts related to job performance. Communicate effectively in the workplace. Identify effective time management skills.
Become and stay informed. Form and express ideas and opinions. Promote family members' growth and development.	Allocate money. Acquire and evaluate data. Understand social and organizational systems. Monitor and correct performance.	Communicate in interpersonal interactions. Communicate personal information. Use leisure time resources. Understand principles of health maintenance.
Become and stay informed. Form and express ideas and opinions. Work together. Take action to strengthen communities. Promote family members' growth and development.	Allocate money. Work on teams. Serve customers. Acquire and evaluate data. Use computers to process information. Understand social and organizational systems. Design or improve systems. Apply technology to specific tasks.	Communicate in interpersonal interactions. Communicate personal information. Use community services. Communicate effectively in the workplace. Understand how technological services work. Interpret information about community problems and their solutions.

To the Teacher

Welcome to *Access Reading!*

Access Reading is a standards-based, four-level reading series for adults and young adults. Each level of *Access Reading* consists of:

• a student book

• an instructor's manual

• an audio tape and audio CD

• a Web site: accessreading.heinle.com

    Access Reading is based on the Equipped for the Future (EFF) Content Standards, the product of a recent comprehensive six-year study delineating "what adults need to know and be able to do in the 21st century." Thus, the reading topics and skills presented in *Access Reading* center around the three key roles adults play throughout their lives identified in the EFF Standards: family member/parent, community member, and worker.

    Access Reading is also compatible with other key skill taxonomies for adult education such as the SCANS Competencies (a U.S. government taxonomy of broad-based skills that workers need to stay competitive in the 21st century) and the CASAS Competencies (a taxonomy of life-skills adults need to live independently in the U.S.), as well as various state standards for adult ESL. A complete correlation to the EFF, SCANS, and CASAS Competencies appears in the Scope and Sequence in the front matter of each *Access Reading* student book.

    The pedagogy of *Access Reading* is based on current, scientifically-based research on reading and on adult learning. Information on the research base of *Access Reading* is in the Instructor's Manual.

The *Access Reading* Student Book

There are 10 thematic units in each student book. Each unit contains two readings. The first reading develops learners' background knowledge and vocabulary, preparing them for the second reading. Each of these readings is based on one of the three adult roles delineated in the EFF Standards. In addition, one of the culminating activities in each unit relates the unit reading and topics to the third adult role in the EFF Standards. For example, in the unit on safety, learners first read about safety rules at work. In the second reading, they learn how to keep their families safe from accidental poisonings. In the culminating activities, they relate this knowledge to community services by learning how to use 9-1-1 to summon appropriate emergency services.

In each unit, learners learn to use a new reading strategy. Throughout each unit, a variety of interactive activities enlivens instruction, and an abundance of exercises checks understanding and ensures that learners are developing target skills and competencies. A unit graphic organizer helps learners develop graphic literacy and reading comprehension skills. A culminating review at the end of each unit allows teachers and learners to determine which skills have been mastered, or whether reteaching or review is necessary to ensure learner success.

Finally, the end matter of each book includes a vocabulary index, a skills index, and a reproducible learning journal.

Teaching a Unit of *Access Reading*

Each unit of *Access Reading* is designed to take four to five class hours to teach. However, it can be expanded through more paired and small group activities, more time for discussion, and more time spent on the activities and exercises.

Use these suggestions as you teach each page of *Access Reading*.

- Have learners talk about the pictures or illustrations on the page.
- Help learners read the directions for each activity.
- Model activities for learners as necessary.
- Allow time for learners to follow the directions and complete each activity.
- Check learner results before going on to the next exercise or activity, providing additional reinforcement as necessary.

Accessing Information

Each unit of *Access Reading* begins with a four-page Accessing Information section.

The one-page unit opener uses pictures and discussion prompts to build interest in and purposes for reading.

- Use the illustrations to develop learners' background knowledge. Have learners identify the people, places, and objects; say what the people are doing; and imagine what the people are saying.

- Use the questions in Talk About It and You Decide to build purposes for learning. Have learners talk over their answers in pairs or small groups and then share their answers with the class.
- Use the skills box to present the unit's goals to learners and to guide your lesson planning throughout the unit.

The second page of Accessing Information begins with a Key Vocabulary section and, in many units, is followed by a reading strategy preview, Before You Read. The Key Vocabulary section develops key vocabulary related to the entire unit. Before You Read is usually a short exercise that allows learners to try the unit's target reading strategy before it is formally presented later in the unit.

- Have learners use background knowledge to brainstorm known vocabulary about the unit topic.
- Have learners use the pictures and illustrations on the page to learn the new vocabulary. Then have learners complete the reinforcement exercise.

The third page of Accessing Information contains the first reading, plus a piece of realia.

- Have learners read the selection and the realia independently.
- Next, play the audio tape/CD as learners follow along silently.
- Before going on to the comprehension exercises on the next page, check comprehension by asking a few simple questions.

In the fourth page of Accessing Information, post-reading exercises check comprehension, develop the unit reading strategy, and allow learners to integrate understanding of the material they just read. In the interactive Teamwork activity, learners use realia to construct meaning, usually using an information gap activity.

Giving Voice

After Accessing Information, a one-page Giving Voice section allows learners to relate the reading topic to their own needs and realities, so that they begin to use their new knowledge to effect meaningful changes in their lives.

Accessing Information

Next, a second three-page Accessing Information section builds toward the unit's second reading. The first page reprises the first reading's content and vocabulary through discussion and a new piece of realia. This page also formally presents the unit's target reading strategy. Use this page to activate learners' prior learning and to orient newcomers or absentees.

- Use peer teaching to ensure that newcomers and absentees have the requisite vocabulary and background knowledge to successfully tackle the reading on the next page.
- Have learners read the unit reading strategy. Clarify as necessary.

The next page contains the second reading.

- Have learners read the selection independently.
- Next, play the audio tape/CD as learners follow along silently.
- Before going on to the comprehension exercises on the next page, check comprehension by asking a few simple questions.

Following the second reading, post-reading exercises check comprehension, develop the unit reading strategy, and allow learners to integrate understanding of the material they read.

Taking Action, Bridging to the Future, and Connection

The Taking Action, Bridging to the Future, and Connection sections bring each unit of ACCESS READING to culmination. In these sections, learners relate the reading topics to the third EFF role not yet covered in the reading and learn skills to apply their new knowledge to their lives.

Enriching Your Vocabulary and Language Note

At key teachable moments throughout ACCESS READING, learners are introduced to a level-appropriate vocabulary development strategy (Enriching Your Vocabulary) and grammar (Language Note) pulled directly from the reading in order to help them read more effectively. Each of these sections is usually followed by a reinforcement activity.

Study Skill

Also at key teachable moments, a Study Skill is presented to help learners improve their learning skills. These study skills are directly related to the content of the unit. For example, in the unit on housing, learners read about creating an area of their homes in which to store all school-related materials.

- Have learners read the information. Clarify as necessary.
- Ask learners to give examples of how they, or other members of their families, might use the suggestion to learn more effectively.

Review

Finally, a one-page Review checks learner understanding of the reading strategy and other skills developed in the unit. Teachers may use this page for review or to ensure learners are ready for the reproducible test in the Instructor's Manual.

- Have learners look over the page for a few minutes. Model the directions if necessary.
- When learners are ready, have them complete the activities. Then check learners' work. Reteach or review as necessary before having the learners complete the reproducible test in the Instructor's Manual.

Your Portfolio

A portfolio assessment activity on the Review page allows teachers to build a portfolio assessment system. A portfolio assessment system allows learners to gather samples of their best work and keep them in a file folder or box. As learners add materials to their portfolios, they will be able to observe growth in their skills and have tangible evidence to document their learning.

- Review each learner's or group's work. Ask learners to say what they learned from the activity, in which areas they want to develop improved skills, and which of their skills have improved over the course of the unit.
- When learners are ready, have them place their completed work in their portfolios.

For more information on setting up a portfolio assessment system, see the *Access Reading* Instructor's Manual.

Summing Up

At the end of each unit, a second skills section reprises the skills presented in the skills box on the unit opener, this time with check-off boxes. Checking off the boxes will provide learners with a sense of pride and accomplishment.

- Help the learners read the skills. Clarify vocabulary as needed.
- Have learners check the boxes that apply to them. Help each learner write a new skill of his or her own on the line and check that box. Check their work. Reteach or review as necessary until all learners can check all the boxes.

Access Reading Instructor's Manual

The *Access Reading* Instructor's Manual contains a complete answer key for exercises in the student book and a complete assessment system. Included in the assessment system are:

• Instructions for setting up a portfolio assessment system.

• Multiple-choice analysis questions to help prepare students for standardized testing.

• Suggestions for ongoing informal assessment throughout each unit.

• Reproducible tests for each unit that give programs and teachers the option of assessing learners formally at regular intervals.

The Instructor's Manual also includes:

• Suggestions for presenting new key vocabulary and structures.

• Complete suggestions for presenting each reading.

• Teaching notes for key exercises and activities.

• Suggestions for previewing and presenting the unit reading strategy.

• Ideas for enriching and enlivening instruction.

Access Reading Web Site

The *Access Reading* Web site contains additional expansion readings and activities. The Web site readings extend the themes presented in the unit readings. The Web site activities can be used as a review and a reinforcement of the skills and vocabulary taught in the student book. The *Access Reading* Web site address is **accessreading.heinle.com.**

Access Reading 1 **Reading Strategies**

Unit 1 (p. 7)   <u>Use pictures and the title to find the main idea.</u>
The main idea is the subject of a reading. Sometimes the pictures and the title can give you an idea of what the reading is about before you start to read. For example, the title "Someone You Should Know" and a photo of Dean Estrada show that the reading is about Dean Estrada.

Unit 2 (p. 17)   <u>Use the first sentence of each paragraph to find the main idea.</u> A good way to find the main idea is to read the first sentence of each paragraph. The main idea helps you understand the rest of the reading. For example, if you read "My family is very nice" and "My name is Mei Chin," you can guess that the main idea is "Mei's family is very nice."

Unit 3 (p. 27)   <u>Scan for specific dates and times.</u> When you read, sometimes you only want to find a date or time. You don't read every word. You just find the information you want. This skill is called *scanning.* If you are reading a memo about a new work bonus plan, you can look over the words quickly and stop to read carefully when you find a date or time.

Unit 4 (p. 37)   <u>Read and draw conclusions.</u> When you read, you often draw conclusions. A conclusion is something you figure out based on the information you have. For example, you are at the supermarket. You see that bread is on sale. You only have a little bread at home, and you eat sandwiches for lunch. So you conclude: It's a good idea to buy some bread on sale.

Unit 5 (p. 47)   <u>Use pictures and captions to find the main idea.</u> The pictures and captions (the words under a picture) can often help you understand the main idea. For example, you see a picture of poinsettia and holly and read the caption "Poinsettia and holly plants are poisonous." You can figure out that the main idea is related to poisons.

Unit 6 (p. 57)   <u>Use background information to help you read.</u> When you read, your background information helps you understand the reading. Using a KWL (K means "know," W means "want to know," and L means "learned.") chart can help you organize this information. For example, when you read about special phone features, you can use what you already know about phones to understand the reading.

Unit 7 (p. 67)   <u>Use related words to help you read.</u> When you read, you will see related words. For example, *Mexico* and *Mexican* are related. *Mexico* is the name of a country. *Mexican* describes someone or something from Mexico. Seeing related words helps you increase your vocabulary.

Unit 8 (p. 77)   <u>Scan for specific information.</u> When you read, you sometimes want to find specific information, such as a price, a phone number, or an address. You don't read every word. You only look for the information you want. This skill is called *scanning.* For example, you want to know if an apartment has free heating. When you read the brochure for the apartment, you look for information about heating.

Unit 9 (p. 87)   <u>Use the context to figure out new words.</u> When you read, you may see new words. When you see a new word, you can use the other words in the sentence to figure out the meaning. For example, look at this sentence:
We ate some delicious krittles at the restaurant last night.
The word *krittle* is not really an English word. But you can figure out what it probably means from the other words in the sentence: *delicious, ate, restaurant.* It must be a kind of food. When you figure out meaning from context, you can read faster and better.

Unit 10 (p. 97)   <u>Read and make inferences.</u> When you make inferences, you use the information you already have to figure out more information. For example, you know Bestway Computers has computer classes. But why does the store have the classes? You figured out the answer: The store has classes so people will buy their computers.

Acknowledgments

Many, many people have contributed to *Access Reading*. First, I would like to acknowledge the individuals at Heinle who made this book possible. I'd like to thank Jim Brown, Sherrise Roehr, and Ingrid Wisniewska for listening to the initial concept, believing in it, and providing constant feedback and support as we developed and tested prototypes and sample units and as the manuscript for each book took shape. I'd also like to acknowledge my gratitude to Yeny Kim for her super editing, constant support, and encouragement during the development of the manuscript. Anita Raducanu's careful management of each stage made the whole editorial process go smoothly. Credit for the design and production go to Lianne Ames of the Heinle production department and Karla Maki and her staff of collaborators at Thompson Steele. Their careful work helped convert the manuscript into the attractive, well laid-out book you hold in your hands today. I'd also like to thank Donna Lee Kennedy of Heinle's marketing department for her help and encouragement throughout the development of this series.

I am also very grateful to the adult educators from around the country who reviewed various stages of the manuscript—invaluable feedback that helped make this book appropriate for classrooms nationwide.

Rocio Castiblanco, *Seminole Community College, Sanford, FL;* Marlon Davis, *Education Service Center, San Antonio, TX;* Renee B. Klosz, *Lindsey Hopkins Technical Educational Center, Miami, FL;* Ronna Magy, *Los Angeles Unified School District, Los Angeles, CA;* David Red, *Fairfax Adult Education, Fairfax, VA*

At National-Louis University, I'd like to thank Leah Miller, Darrell Bloom, Bernadette Herman, Diane Salmon, Alison Hilsabeck, and Elizabeth Hawthorne for not only encouraging me to write, but also for helping me carve out the time from my other responsibilities to write this series.

I'd also like to express my appreciation to Mary Jane Maples, who taught me so many of the skills I used in writing this book. I also owe a debt of gratitude to Bob Wilson for his advice and guidance over the years.

Finally, I'd like to thank my parents for giving me the gift of reading. I hope that through this book adult learners gain the reading skills that they need to reach their hopes, goals, and dreams.

Photo Credits

ix top: ©Walter Hodges/CORBIS; c: ©Ed Eckstein/CORBIS; b: ©PhotoDisc/Getty Images

Unit 1
2 left: ©Ariel Skelley/CORBIS; tr: Courtesy of the author; br: ©Mark Peterson/CORBIS SABA. 4 Courtesy of the author. 8 ©Mug Shots/CORBIS. 10 ©Michael Newman/Photo Edit. 11 ©Heinle

Unit 2
12 left: ©David Young-Wolff/Photo Edit; tr: ©Rob Lewine/ CORBIS; br: ©Gaetano/CORBIS. 15 ©Gary Conner/Index Stock Imagery. 16 ©Ariel Skelley/CORBIS

Unit 3
21 ©Heinle. 22 left: ©Alan Schein Photography/CORBIS; tr: ©Michael Newman/Photo Edit; br: ©Tom & Dee Ann McCarthy/CORBIS. 23 ©Will & Deni McIntyre/CORBIS

Unit 4
32 left: ©Ariel Skelley/CORBIS; tr: ©Spencer Grant/Photo Edit; br: ©Dwayne Newton/Photo Edit

Unit 5
42 left: ©Michael Keller/Index Stock Imagery; tr: ©Amy Etra/Photo Edit; br: ©Omni Photo Communications/Index Stock Imagery

Unit 6
52 left: ©David Young-Wolff/Photo Edit; tr and br: ©Stewart Cohen/Index Stock Imagery. 57 ©Grantpix/Index Stock Imagery. 60 ©Eyewire/Getty

Unit 7
62 left: ©Jeff Greenberg/Photo Edit; tr: ©David Young-Wolff/ Photo Edit; br: ©Greg Gibson/Associated Press/AP. 63 tl: ©Tom Carter/Photo Edit; tr: ©Jonathan Nourok/Photo Edit; bl: ©Steve Dunwell/Index Stock Imagery; br: ©Jon Feingersh/CORBIS. 64 top: Mural by Florin Durzynski, 1940. WPA mural; from the Chicago Public Schools Permanent Art collection; bottom: "*Heroes of Mexico Project,*" directed by Francisco G. Mendoza and the Orozco Students, 1993-1994, Orozco Academy, Chicago. Photo by Heidi Brady/Odyssey/Chicago. 66-67 ©Wendy Ennes. 68 tr: ©Bettmann/CORBIS; c: ©Bettmann/Corbis; br: Courtesy of the Women's Polish Alliance

Unit 8
71: ©Associated Press, The Honolulu Advertiser. 72 left: ©Michael Newman/Photo Edit; tr: ©Amy Etra/Photo Edit; br: ©Tom Carter/Photo Edit

Unit 9
82 left: ©David Young-Wolff/Photo Edit; tr: ©Myrleen Cate/Index Stock Imagery; br: ©Mack 2 Stock Exchange/Index Stock Imagery

Unit 10
92 left: ©Cindy Charles/Photo Edit; tr: ©Michael Newman/Photo Edit; br: ©Richard Orton/Index Stock Imagery. 98 All ©Heinle; 2nd from top: ©Lonnie Duka/Index Stock Imagery. 101 ©Heinle.

To the Learner

Your Job

Welcome to *Access Reading!*

This book will help you learn to read better. In this book, you will read about all parts of your life—in your job, your community, and your family.

You will learn many things in this book. You will learn to read more quickly. You will learn vocabulary. You will learn grammar. You will learn study skills. You will learn speaking skills.

What do you want to learn from this book? Check the box or boxes. Then follow the instructions.

What do you want to learn? I want to	Instructions
☐ 1. Improve my vocabulary.	Pay attention to the Key Vocabulary and Enriching Your Vocabulary sections.
☐ 2. Improve my reading skills.	Pay attention to the Reading Strategy sections.
☐ 3. Improve my grammar.	Pay attention to the Language Note sections.
☐ 4. Improve my study skills.	Pay attention to the Study Skill sections.
☐ 5. Use new information to improve my life.	Pay attention to the Giving Voice, Taking Action, Connection and Bridging to the Future sections.
☐ 6. Improve my speaking skills.	Pay attention to the Talk About It, Talk It Over, Teamwork, and You Decide sections.
☐ 7. Check my learning.	Pay attention to the Review page and the Portfolio activity.

Your Community

Your Family

Getting Along

In this unit, you will:

1. Read about people at school.
2. Read about making friends.
3. Use pictures and the title to find the main idea.
4. Understand subject pronouns.
5. Use listing.

 Accessing Information

Talk About It

Where are the people? What are they doing? What are they talking about? Which ones are friends? How do you know?

You Decide

How do people find new friends? Work with a partner. In your notebook, write a list.

Key Vocabulary

A. In this unit, you will read about school and new friends. First, work with a partner. Which words are about school? Circle the words. Then add words of your own.

(teacher)   _____

neighbor   _____

homework   _____

class   _____

police officer   _____

B. Look at the pictures. Work with your partner. Take turns pointing at the pictures and saying the words.

Metalworking   **Computers**   **Keyboarding**

EXERCISE 1   Vocabulary
A. Look at the list. What do people study in adult schools? Circle.

(English)	computers	Spanish
cooking	sleeping	math
walking	reading	child care
metalworking	eating	office skills

B. What do you want to study? Tell your partner. What does your partner want to study? Tell the class.

EXERCISE 2   Before You Read

Look at the reading. Don't read it. Just look at the picture and the title. What is the reading about? Circle.

a student at an adult school   a teacher at an adult school

the head of an adult school   the cafeteria at an adult school

Who's in charge of the adult school?

TRACK 1

dean = the head of a school or college

Dr. Estrada

Someone You Should Know

Dr. Ricardo Estrada is the dean of an adult school in Chicago. About 2,800 students study there. Students are from Mexico, China, Poland, Russia, and Lithuania. Students can study English, office skills, metalworking, and other subjects. Then they can get good jobs.

Dean Ricardo Estrada

Dr. Estrada came to Chicago from Colombia in 1979. He had several problems. He didn't have much money, he didn't have a job, and he didn't know English. First, he got a job in a restaurant. He was a dishwasher, but he studied English during the day in an adult school. Then he studied English and business in a college.

College was difficult for him. He was the only Colombian student, so he felt very lonely. He made friends with five other students. They studied together, and finally he finished school. He got a job at a university in Chicago.

Dr. Estrada is a good dean because he understands the students' problems and helps them. He likes helping people.

ESL

Class Title	Time & Location		
English as a Second Language 1	Monday & Wednesday	10:00 AM to 12:00 PM	Room 214
	Monday & Wednesday	7:00 PM to 9:00 PM	Room 216
	Tuesday & Thursday	9:00 AM to 11:00 AM	Room 211
	Tuesday & Thursday	7:00 PM to 9:00 PM	Room 109

EXERCISE 3   After You Read

Work with a partner. Circle the answer.

1. Look at your answer to Exercise 2 on page 4. Was your answer correct?   YES   NO

2. The main idea is what an article is generally about. What's the main idea of the article?
   a. Dr. Estrada has a nice family.
   b. Dr. Estrada's school is very good.
   c. Dr. Estrada is a good dean because he understands students.

EXERCISE 4   Yes or No

Write **yes** or **no** on the line.

___yes___   **1.** Dr. Estrada is the dean of an adult school.

_____   **2.** At Dr. Estrada's school, students study office skills.

_____   **3.** Dr. Estrada had problems when he was a student.

_____   **4.** Dr. Estrada had a lot of money when he was a student.

_____   **5.** Students from the school can find good jobs.

_____   **6.** Dr. Estrada is good at his job.

Enriching Your Vocabulary

People study many subjects, such as English. Look at the reading. Circle the subjects people study.

EXERCISE 5   Subjects in School

Look at the pictures. What are the people studying? Match. Write the letter on the line.

1. _____
2. _____
3. _____

a. car repair
b. English
c. metalworking
d. office occupations

Teamwork

Work with a partner. Student A looks at the class schedule on page 4. Student B looks at his or her schedule on page 102. When can Student B study English? Help Student B find a class that works with his or her schedule. Then switch roles and repeat the activity.

Giving Voice

Talk It Over

A. At first, Dean Estrada had problems in the U.S. Look at the list of problems. Which problems did Dean Estrada have? Which problems do you worry about?

	Dean Estrada	Me
1. need money	☐	☐
2. need a good job	☐	☐
3. need more time for school	☐	☐
4. feel lonely	☐	☐
5. need a good car	☐	☐
6. children are lonely	☐	☐
7. need a house or apartment	☐	☐
8. need special clothes for work	☐	☐
9. _____	☐	☐
10. _____	☐	☐

I need child care.

B. Share your list with a partner. What problems do you and your partner worry about? In your notebook, make a list.

EXERCISE 6   Finding Solutions

A. Think about your list of problems in Talk It Over. Where can you get help? In your notebook, write a list of questions for a counselor.

B. Go over your list of questions with your teacher. Then meet with a counselor. Ask your questions. How can you get help? Write down the counselor's answers. Share the answers with the class.

STUDY SKILL
Find a Study Buddy

A study buddy is someone who helps you when you study. Dr. Estrada had problems with school. Then he found some study buddies. They helped him with his studies.

A study buddy should be someone in your class. You can ask your study buddy for help. Your study buddy can call you if you are absent from school. Find a study buddy in your class. Then work together outside of class.

Accessing Information

Talk About It

Look at the cover of the booklet. What is Citywide Adult School? What do the pictures and words tell you about the school? Do you want to study there? Why or why not?

READING STRATEGY
Use Pictures and the Title to Find the Main Idea

When you read, you often want to find out the main idea. The main idea is the general topic of the reading. You can often find the main idea from pictures, the title, and key words.

EXERCISE 7   Before You Read

Look at the article on the next page. Before you read, use the picture and the title to figure out the main idea. Write a few words on the line.

_____

How do you find friends in a new city?

Chen Li is from China. Now she lives in Houston. Her husband is the manager of a supermarket. She stays at home with their two children. The children are 2 years old and 4 years old. Chen is lonely a lot. She wants more friends.

Chen likes to read magazines. She read this article about making friends in a new city.

TRACK 2

Making Friends After You Move

YOU ARE NEW IN YOUR CITY, and you feel sad. You think about your friends and family in your old home. How can you make friends in your new home? Here are some answers.

Where can I meet new friends?
Most people meet friends at work. People also find friends at school and at religious organizations. So talk to people at work. Talk to people at school. Talk to people at your children's school. If you are religious, join a religious organization. Go to programs at parks and libraries.

My English isn't very good. How can I meet people?
You are studying English now, so that is a good first step. To learn social English, watch TV and movies. Then speak English at work and school. People will hear you, and they will talk to you.

People aren't very friendly. What can I do?
You are new in town, so *you* need to be friendly. Smile. Say "Hello" or "Good Morning" at work and school. Stop and talk to people in the hall or the break room. Talk with other students before and after school.

I don't have anything to talk about with people. What can I talk about?
Americans talk about the weather a lot. They also talk about TV programs, movies, and sports. So watch TV. Check the weather report. Then talk about TV and the weather with people. Do you like sports? Watch some games on the weekend. Talk about them on Monday.

Remember, good friends are hard to find. It takes time to find a true friend.

EXERCISE 8   After You Read

Answer the questions. Circle.

1. What's the main idea of the article?
 a. ways to meet friends in a new place
 b. ways to solve your problems
 c. ways to find friends for your children

2. Look at your answer to Exercise 7 on page 7. Was your answer
correct?   YES   NO

EXERCISE 9   New Friends

How can the people find friends? Match. Write the letter on the line.

_____C_____ **1.** Soo is taking a computer
course.

_____ **2.** Pablo always looks worried.

_____ **3.** Felicia doesn't speak English.

_____ **4.** Tony loves sports.

_____ **5.** Tuyet likes to read.

a. Join a book club at the library.
b. Smile at people.
c. Talk to the other students in the class.
d. Study English at an adult school.
e. Join a team at the park.

EXERCISE 10   Subject Pronouns

Look at page 8. Find a sentence with each pronoun. Write the
sentence. Then write the word that matches the pronoun.

Pronoun	Sentence from Page 8	The Person Who Matches the Pronoun
she	Now she lives in Houston.	Chen Li
1. she		
2. you		
3. they		

LANGUAGE NOTE
Subject Pronouns

The readings in this unit
use subject pronouns.
Understanding subject
pronouns will help you
improve your reading
skills.

Words like **he, she,** and **it**
are pronouns. A pronoun
takes the place of a noun.

Dean Estrada is the
head of an adult school.
He is the head of an
adult school.

Chen Li is lonely in the
United States.
She's lonely in the United
States.

Talk to neighbors.

👉 Taking Action

A. You want to make more friends. What do you do? In your notebook, write a list.

B. Show your list to a partner. Talk over your lists. Add more ideas to your list.

C. Work with a group. Read your list aloud. Make a group list.

🌉 Bridging to the Future

A. Work with a partner. You are at family night at school. Your partner is another parent. Get to know your partner. Create a conversation.

B. Work with a small group. Present your conversation to the group. Listen to the other students' conversations.

Example:

Parent A: Does your daughter, Lisa, like her math class?

Parent B: No, it's very difficult. I help her with the homework.

🔗 Workplace Connection

Work with a group to solve this problem.

George Hartley works at your company. He does not have many friends at work. People say, "George is not very nice. He doesn't talk to anyone."

Help George. How can he get more friends at work? Talk over your ideas. Then share your ideas with the class. Use everyone's ideas to create a class list.

Review

An Excellent Teacher

Teacher Linda Bates of Allentown Adult School

Linda Bates is a teacher at Allentown Adult School. She was an English teacher in Colombia and Thailand. At Allentown Adult School, she teaches English as a second language. Students say, "Ms. Bates is a very good teacher. She works very hard." Students like her classes. They say, "Her classes are interesting. We learn a lot from her."

EXERCISE 11 The Main Idea

Use the picture and title to figure out the main idea. Circle the letter.
a. Linda Bates has a lot of experience.
b. Linda Bates is a good teacher.
c. Linda Bates is from Allentown.

EXERCISE 12 Yes or No

Write **yes** or **no** on the line.

_____ **1.** Linda Bates is a good teacher.

_____ **2.** Linda Bates teaches computer classes.

_____ **3.** Linda Bates taught in Colombia and Thailand.

_____ **4.** Students learn a lot in her classes.

Your Portfolio

A portfolio is a collection of good work. In this book, you will put some of your work in your portfolio at the end of every unit.

Work with a group. Look at your list of ideas about making friends from Taking Action on page 10. In your group, make a list of the five best ways to make friends. Put your list in your portfolio.

Summing Up

I can:

☐ **1.** Read about people at school.

☐ **2.** Read about making friends.

☐ **3.** Use pictures and the title to find the main idea.

☐ **4.** Understand subject pronouns.

☐ **5.** Use listing.

☐ **6.** _____

Around Town

In this unit, you will:

1. Read about families.
2. Read about community workers.
3. Use the first sentence of each paragraph to find the main idea.
4. Use **a** and **an** with occupations.
5. Use a chart to organize information.

 Accessing Information

Talk About It

Where are the people? What are they doing? Who is working? Where do they work?

You Decide

Are families important? Why? Tell your partner. Then share your partner's ideas with the class.

Key Vocabulary

A. In this unit you are going to read about families and community workers. Work with a partner. Look at the pictures. In your notebook, write two lists: people in a family and people who work in a community. Follow the example.

Family	Community
father	mail carrier

B. Work with a partner. Look at the pictures. Find these people in the pictures.

mother, father, sister, brother, son, daughter, wife, husband, grandfather, grandmother, mail carrier, firefighter, police officer

EXERCISE 1   Vocabulary
Which word doesn't belong? Cross it off.

1. grandmother   ~~brother~~   mother
2. firefighter   grandfather   police officer
3. mother   son   police officer
4. grandmother   mother   son
5. father   brother   grandmother
6. police officer   family   firefighter

EXERCISE 2   Before You Read
Read the first sentence of each paragraph. What is the article about? Write a few words in your notebook.

What's Mei's family like?

Mei Chin is a student at an adult school in San Francisco. She wrote about her family.

TRACK 3

My family is very nice. We're from Hong Kong, but we live in San Francisco now. We moved to the United States in 1997.

My name is Mei Chin. I live with my mother and my father. I work in the morning, and I go to school in the afternoon. I study English and computers. In my free time, I watch movies. I also cook and help my parents at home.

My mother and father are very nice. My father's name is Liang. My mother's name is Sung. They have a bookstore. I work in the bookstore with them every morning.

I have two brothers. Byron is my little brother. He's 13. He's in middle school. He's a very good student. He's good at baseball and soccer. In his free time he reads and plays video games.

My big brother's name is Han, but we call him Henry. He's married. His wife is from Hong Kong, too. Her name is Wan. Henry and Wan have a son and a daughter. Their names are Ming and Fang. They live in Los Angeles. Henry is an engineer. His wife is a clerk in a bank. Ming and Fang go to elementary school. In their free time, they play soccer. They say that they want to work in our bookstore with their grandfather, grandmother, and aunt!

Chin's Imported Books
English and Chinese Books
Magazines and Newspapers from China

Hours
Monday to Friday 9:00 AM to 9:00 PM
Saturday   9:00 AM to 5:00 PM
Sunday   Closed

122 W. Union Street
San Francisco, CA 94112
(650) 555-1227

EXERCISE 3 After You Read

Work with a partner. Talk over your answer to
Exercise 2 on page 14. Was your answer correct?
Share your ideas with the class.

EXERCISE 4 Answer the Questions

Answer each question in a few words. Write
your answers in your notebook.

1. Where does Mei live?

2. Where do Mei's mother and father work?

3. How many brothers does Mei have?

4. Who is Byron?

5. How many children do Henry and Wan have?

6. How many people in the family go to school?

Enriching Your Vocabulary

Words such as **father** and **aunt** show family relationships. Work
with a partner. Look at the reading. Circle the family words.

EXERCISE 5 Family Relationships

A. Mei's father needs to complete an
insurance form. Complete the form for him.
One person's name is missing. Write the
name on the form.

B. In your notebook, make a chart about
your family. Use the chart in A as a model.

Golden Gate Insurance Company

Family Members Covered Under This Plan
(Family members must be age 23 or younger and live with you.)

Name	Relationship	Age
Liang Chin	yourself	46
Sung Chin		42
Mei Chin		19

Teamwork

Work with a partner. Student A looks at the business card on
page 14. Student B looks at the business card on page 102. Ask
questions about Student B's business card and complete the chart.
Answer Student B's questions about your business card. Then
switch roles and repeat the activity.

What's the name of the business?	
What city is it in?	
What does it sell?	
Does it sell magazines?	
Is it open on Sunday?	

Giving Voice

Talk It Over

A. What is your family like? In your notebook, write a few sentences about your family.

My family is small.

B. Work with a partner. Read your sentences to your partner. What is your partner's family like? Tell the class.

EXERCISE 6   Strong Families

A. Mei's family is strong and happy. Why are they strong and happy? Work with a partner. Check the boxes. Then add more ideas.

☐ **1.** Mei goes to adult school.

☐ **2.** The family has insurance.

☐ **3.** Byron works in a bank after school.

☐ **4.** Mr. and Mrs. Chin work in their bookstore.

☐ **5.** Byron plays soccer after school.

☐ **6.** Mei is a teacher in an adult school.

☐ **7.** _____

☐ **8.** _____

Eat dinner together.

B. You want to make your family strong and happy. What do you do to make your family strong and happy? In your notebook, write three ideas. Then talk over your ideas with your partner. Add more ideas to your list.

Accessing Information

Talk About It

On a field trip, children visit a place outside of school. Look at the
notice about the field trip. Circle the words that describe families.
Underline the words for community workers.

Washington School

Dear Parents,
Your son or daughter is invited on a field trip on Thursday, September 19. Our class will visit the Green Street Fire
Station. We will meet firefighters and ambulance drivers. The class will learn about fire safety. If it's OK for your
child to go on the field trip, please sign the permission slip.

- - - - - - - - - ✂ - ✂ - - - - - -

Permission Slip

My son or daughter, _____Roberto Espinoza_____, has my permission to go on a field trip to the Green
Street Fire Station on Thursday, September 19.

Signed: _____Max Espinoza_____
                    Mother or Father

READING STRATEGY
**Use the First Sentence of Each Paragraph
to Find the Main Idea**

The main idea is the subject of a reading. A good way to find the main idea is to
read the first sentence of each paragraph. The main idea helps you understand the
rest of the reading.

EXERCISE 7   Using the First Sentence of Each Paragraph

Work with a partner. Look at the article on page 18. Read only the
questions and the first sentence of each answer. Underline the first
sentence of each answer. What is the main idea? Write a few
words on the line.

What do you do in a fire?

Police officers, mail carriers, and firefighters help everyone in the community. Sometimes, these workers help people in special ways. Read the article about Frank LoCasio. He helps children every day.

Someone You Should Know
Firefighter Teaches Children Fire Safety

Frank LoCasio is a very special firefighter. Every day he talks to groups of children about fire safety. LoCasio, a firefighter for 25 years, spoke to us about his work.

Who do you talk to?
I talk to groups of children at school. Every day I talk to children at a different school. Last year I spoke at over 100 schools to 15,000 children. Sometimes groups of children come to the fire station. Then I show them the fire trucks and ambulances.

Why is talking to children important?
It's important because many children are hurt or die in fires. In the U.S., about 1,100 children die in fires each year. That's about three children each day. And every year, 3,600 children are hurt in fires.

What do you tell the children?
I show pictures of fires. I explain why fires are dangerous. Then I give four rules:

1. Don't play with fire.

2. Make sure that your home has smoke alarms with batteries.

3. Know how to get out of your house and school in case of fire.

4. When a fire starts, go outside. Then call 911.

Do you like your work?
Yes, it's important work, and it helps people. Here is a thank-you letter I got last week from a family. I spoke to the children in the family last year. Last month they had a fire. They all escaped. So the father wrote me a letter.

Please read us part of the letter.
OK. "Thanks to you, our family is safe today. After your talk, my children said, 'We need a smoke alarm.' So we bought one. When the fire started, the smoke alarm rang. We all went outside, and I called the fire department. Our house was badly burned, but we are OK. Thank you very much!"

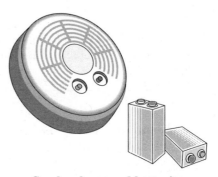

Smoke alarm and batteries

EXERCISE 8   Using the First Sentence of Each Paragraph

Read the first sentence of each of Frank's answers. Then circle the answer below.

1. What is the main idea of the article?
   a. Frank LoCasio is a firefighter who helps keep children safe.
   b. Frank LoCasio is a firefighter.
   c. Frank LoCasio's safety rules helped a family last month.
   d. Four safety rules help you stay safe.

2. Look at your answer to Exercise 7 on page 17. Was your answer correct?   YES   NO

EXERCISE 9   Yes or No

Read the sentences. Write **yes** or **no** on the line.

_____ 1. Frank LoCasio is a new firefighter.

_____ 2. Frank LoCasio talks to children about fire safety.

_____ 3. A lot of children die in fires in the U.S.

_____ 4. Frank LoCasio wants to start fires.

_____ 5. Frank's advice helps children.

LANGUAGE NOTE
A and An with Occupations

The reading on Frank LoCasio uses **a** and **an**. Understanding **a** and **an** will help you improve your reading skills. When you say or write an occupation (job), use **a** or **an**. Use **an** before jobs that start with **a, e, i, o,** or **u**.

   Henry's **an** engineer.

Use **a** for all other jobs.

   Frank's **a** firefighter.

EXERCISE 10   A or An

Write A, a, An, or an on the line.

1. Please call _____ police officer.

2. _____ firefighter is talking to the children at school.

3. Juan is _____ ambulance driver.

4. I am studying to be _____ computer engineer.

5. Mr. Acosta is _____ teacher.

6. Ms. Lee is _____ engineer.

Taking Action

A. Who are the community workers who help you? How do you call them for help? Complete the chart. Use a phone directory to help you.

Service	Worker	Phone Number
ambulance	ambulance driver	911
fire department		
police department		
school		

B. You should call 911 only in an emergency. Call when there is a fire. Call when a crime is happening. Call when someone is badly hurt. Look at the problems. Should you call 911? Check the boxes.

☐ **1.** Your mail is late.

☐ **2.** There is a fire next door.

☐ **3.** You have a bad headache.

☐ **4.** Your boss cut her hand at work. The cut is very bad.

☐ **5.** There was a big car accident. Seven people are hurt.

Bridging to the Future

A. Work with a partner. Take turns pretending to call 911. Follow the example. Use the problems you checked above.

B. Work with a group. Present your conversation to the group. Listen to the other students' conversations.

A: 911. What's your emergency?
B: There's a fire next door.
A: What's the address?
B: 300 Bridge Street
A: OK. The fire department will be there right away.

Workplace Connection

Work with a group to solve this problem.

Frank LoCasio helps a lot of people at work. What can we do at work to help others at work? For example, a cook can tell the manager that something is dangerous. What can you do at your workplace or school? Share your ideas with the class. Use everyone's ideas to create a class list.

Review

EXERCISE 11   What's the Main Idea?

Read the first sentence of each paragraph of the reading below. Then circle the letter of the main idea.

a. Ramona Vilar is from Cuba.

b. Ramona Vilar has a nice family.

c. Ramona's husband is in Cuba, but Ramona is in Miami.

d. Ramona wants to move to Cuba.

Ramona Vilar is from Cuba. She came to the United States in 1996 with her children. She's 35 years old. She has a good job in Miami. She works in a supermarket. First, she was a clerk. Now she's an assistant manager. She likes her job a lot. The pay is good and her boss is very nice.

Ramona's husband is a doctor. His name is Pablo. He's 37. Now he's in Cuba. He works in a large hospital in Havana. He wants to come to the United States next year to work in a hospital in Miami.

Ramona's two children are good students. Her son, Edgar, is in middle school. He's 13. He likes reading and soccer. Her daughter, Marta, is very young. She's 7. She's in first grade. She likes to play with her friends.

Ramona and her children like Miami a lot. Her children are in good schools, and she has a good job. They have a lot of nice friends. They will be really happy when her husband moves to Miami.

Your Portfolio

Look at the chart you made in Exercise 5, Part B on page 15. Use the information to write a few sentences about your family. Put your sentences in your portfolio.

Summing Up

I can:

☐ **1.** Read about families.

☐ **2.** Read about community workers.

☐ **3.** Use the first sentence of each paragraph to find the main idea.

☐ **4.** Use **a** and **an** with occupations.

☐ **5.** Use a chart to organize information.

☐ **6.** _____

Keeping Busy

Accessing Information

Talk About It

What are the people doing? Why? Why are they thinking about the time?

You Decide

Everyone is busy these days. Why are you busy? How do you keep track of your schedule?

Key Vocabulary

A. In this unit, you are going to read about time and dates. Work with a partner. In your notebook, write all of the time words and expressions you know.

B. Look at the calendar. Study the vocabulary.

January 2003						
Sun	Mon	Tue	Wed	Thu	Fri	Sat
			1	2	3	4
5	6	7	8	9	10	11
12	13	14	15	16	17	18
19	20	21	22	23	24	25
26	27	28	29	30	31	

Months	Days
January	Sunday
February	Monday
March	Tuesday
April	Wednesday
May	Thursday
June	Friday
July	Saturday
August	
September	
October	
November	
December	

To write the date in English, we write:

November 2, 2004

EXERCISE 1   Vocabulary

A. Answer the questions.

1. What day is it today? _____

2. What's today's date? _____

3. What is your date of birth? _____

B. What's an important date for you? Your birthday? The day you moved to a new place? Why is it important? Tell your partner. Then listen to your partner. Share your partner's date with the class.

EXERCISE 2 Before You Read

Read the questions. Look at the memo to find the answer. Then circle the letter.

1. When did Tony Rizzo write the memo?
    a. September 21, 2004
    b. September 27, 2004

2. When does the new policy begin?
    a. September 21, 2004
    b. September 27, 2004

 How do you get a bonus at work?

TRACK 5

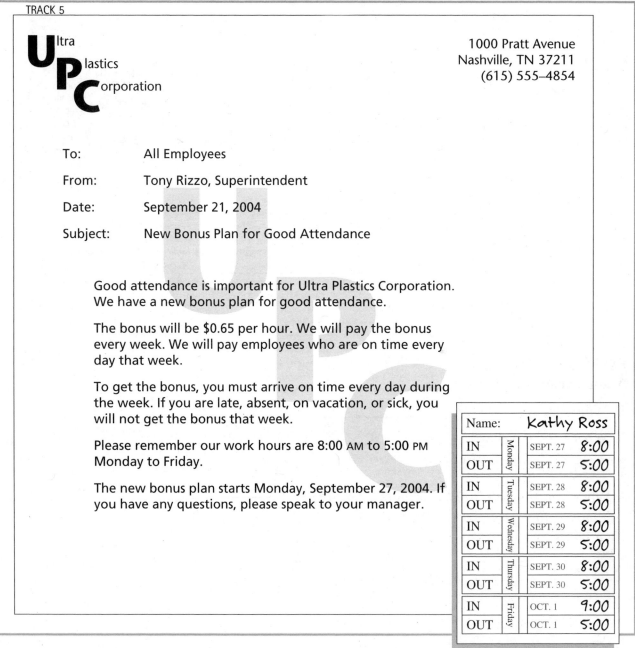

UPC
Ultra
Plastics
Corporation

1000 Pratt Avenue
Nashville, TN 37211
(615) 555–4854

To: All Employees

From: Tony Rizzo, Superintendent

Date: September 21, 2004

Subject: New Bonus Plan for Good Attendance

Good attendance is important for Ultra Plastics Corporation. We have a new bonus plan for good attendance.

The bonus will be $0.65 per hour. We will pay the bonus every week. We will pay employees who are on time every day that week.

To get the bonus, you must arrive on time every day during the week. If you are late, absent, on vacation, or sick, you will not get the bonus that week.

Please remember our work hours are 8:00 AM to 5:00 PM Monday to Friday.

The new bonus plan starts Monday, September 27, 2004. If you have any questions, please speak to your manager.

Name:		Kathy Ross	
IN	Monday	SEPT. 27	**8:00**
OUT		SEPT. 27	**5:00**
IN	Tuesday	SEPT. 28	**8:00**
OUT		SEPT. 28	**5:00**
IN	Wednesday	SEPT. 29	**8:00**
OUT		SEPT. 29	**5:00**
IN	Thursday	SEPT. 30	**8:00**
OUT		SEPT. 30	**5:00**
IN	Friday	OCT. 1	**9:00**
OUT		OCT. 1	**5:00**

EXERCISE 3 Yes or No

Write **yes** or **no** on the line.

_____ **1.** The new bonus plan is for good attendance.

_____ **2.** The bonus is $0.56 per hour.

_____ **3.** To get the bonus, you have to be on time every day
for a month.

_____ **4.** To get the bonus, you have to be on time every day
for a week.

_____ **5.** If you are sick for one day, you will get a bonus.

_____ **6.** If you are absent, you **don't** get a bonus.

EXERCISE 4 Kathy Ross

Look at Kathy's time card on page 24.
Answer the questions in your notebook.

1. Was Kathy at work every day?

2. Was Kathy on time every day?

3. Will Kathy get a bonus? Why or why not?

Enriching Your Vocabulary

AM and PM describe times of day.

AM   From 12:00 midnight to 11:59 in
the morning

PM   From 12:00 noon to 11:59 at night

Look at the memo again. Circle AM and PM.

LANGUAGE NOTE
It's + the Time

The reading on a work bonus plan uses times.
Understanding how to express time will help you
improve your reading skills.

Look at how we write and say the time:

We say:	We write:
seven seven o'clock	7:00
seven thirty	7:30
seven fifty-three	7:53

To say the time, we use **It's** + the time.

What time is it?
It's three o'clock.

Teamwork

Work with a partner. Student A looks at Kathy Ross's time card on
page 24. Student B looks at Frank Stover's time card on page 103.
Ask Student B the questions about Frank Stover. Write the answers
in your notebook. Answer Student B's questions about Kathy Ross.
Then switch roles and repeat the activity.

1. What time does Frank usually start work?

2. Was Frank late to work this week?

3. Was Frank absent this week? Why?

4. Did Frank work late this week? What day?

5. Should Frank get the bonus this week? Why or why not?

Giving Voice

EXERCISE 5   Late for Work

A. Look at the list of reasons for being late. Which are good reasons? Which are bad reasons? Write the numbers in the boxes. Add two reasons of your own.

Reasons for Being Late

1. You got up late.

2. You had to take your car to the mechanic.

3. You were talking to your friends in the parking lot.

4. You needed to talk to your children's teachers.

5. You needed to do your homework for English class.

6. You were eating breakfast in the break room.

7. The bus was late.

8. You were at a party late last night.

9. _____

10. _____

Good Reasons	Bad Reasons
	1,

B. Share your answers with your partner. Do you agree? Why or why not?

Talk It Over

Work with a small group. You work at Ultra Plastics Corporation. You are talking over the bonus plan with your coworkers. Is the plan fair? Why do you think so? Look at the good reasons for being late in Exercise 5. Will workers with those reasons get the bonus? Is that fair? Why or why not? Share your answers with the class.

Accessing Information

Talk About It

Check number: **12345** ID number: **678**	Ultra Plastics Corporation		Pay period September 27 to October 1
Name	**GROSS PAY**		
Antonio Fajardo	Hours	Rate	Amount
	40	$9.00	$360
	40	$0.65	$26

Check number: **12364** ID number: **324**	Ultra Plastics Corporation		Pay period September 27 to October 1
Name	**GROSS PAY**		
Kathy Ross	Hours	Rate	Amount
	39	$9.00	$351

What information can you find on the pay stubs? Who got the bonus? Who didn't get the bonus? Why? If necessary, review page 24.

 READING STRATEGY
Scan for Specific Dates and Times

When you read, sometimes you only want to find a date or time. You don't read every word. You just find the information you want. This strategy is called **scanning**.

EXERCISE 6 Scan for Specific Dates and Times

Look at Kathy Ross's time card on page 24. What time did she start work on Wednesday? What date was Friday?

EXERCISE 7 Scanning

Scan Kathy Ross's appointment book below. Write the days and times of the activities.

1. Go to work. _____

2. Go to the supermarket. _____

3. Go to the movies. _____

Why was Kathy late for work on Friday?

Kathy Ross and her husband, Michael, are very busy. Look at Kathy's appointment book for two days this week.

TRACK 6

Friday, October 1		Saturday, October 2	
8:00 AM	Take car to mechanic	8:00 AM	Take Monica to soccer practice
9:00 AM	Work	9:00 AM	Supermarket, dry cleaner, drug store
12:00 PM	Call Monica's teacher, (615)555-4190	12:00 PM	Pick up Monica from soccer practice
		1:30 PM	Dr. Martin
	Call mechanic about car, (615)555-6789		
		3:00 PM	Mall—buy school clothes for Monica
5:00 PM	Leave work		
6:00 PM	Pick up car	6:00 PM	Take Monica to Nancy Chen's house
8:00 PM	Dinner with Michael	8:00 PM	See movie "Always Tomorrow" with Michael

EXERCISE 8   Checking the Appointment Book

Scan Kathy's appointment book to answer the questions.

1. Why was Kathy late to work on Friday? _____

_____

2. When are the activities? Write the days and times.

    a. Take Monica to soccer practice. _____

    b. Have dinner with Michael. _____

    c. Go to the mall. _____

You have an appointment

Name: __Kathy Ross__

Date: __October 2__

Time: __1:00__

Rob Martin, D.D.S.
10 Lake Street
Nashville, Tennessee 37210

For cancellations, call (615) 555-1234

3. Look at the appointment card. What time is Kathy's appointment? Is Kathy's appointment book correct? Correct her appointment book.

4. Look at the movie schedule below. What time does Kathy want to go to the movies? What movie does she want to see? Check her appointment book. Where can she see the movie? Circle the name of the theater.

▐ Broadway Cinema				
3201 Broadway				
Always Tomorrow				
1:00	3:00	5:00	7:00	9:00
Today's the Day				
2:00	4:00	6:00	8:00	10:00

▐ Music City Mall Cineplex				
Car Race 3				
1:30	3:30	5:30	7:30	9:30
Always Tomorrow				
2:00	4:00	6:00	8:00	10:00

Taking Action

Complete the appointment book with your schedule for today.

Time	Appointments

STUDY SKILL
Use an Appointment Book

Do you forget to do your homework? Use an appointment book or calendar. Write down the time you want to do your homework. Write down the times you have school, too.

Bridging to the Future

Work with a partner. Take turns telling your boss why you were late. Then present your conversations to the class.

A: Sorry I was late, Mr. Bloom. I had some car trouble this morning.

B: No problem, Kathy. Try to be here on time tomorrow.

A: Thanks, Mr. Bloom.

Activity:
Conference
at school
Date:
November 1
Time: 3:00

Community Connection

People have many community activities. They go to meetings at school. They go to meetings at religious organizations. Work with a group. In your notebook, write down your community activities.

Review

EXERCISE 9   Scanning

Scan Alvin's appointment book to answer the questions.

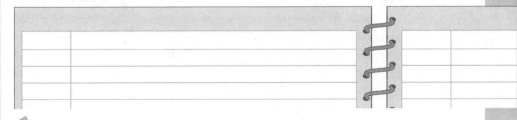

Tuesday, May 2		Wednesday, May 3
9:00	Go to the post office	
10:00	Start work	
2:00	Leave work. Drive home.	
3:00	Study English	
5:00	Cook dinner for family	
7:00	English class	

1. What date is the list for? _____

2. What will Alvin do at 2:00? _____

3. Alvin is studying English right now. What time is it? _____

EXERCISE 10   Your Schedule

What are you doing tomorrow? Complete the appointment book.
Write the date, too.

Your Portfolio

Look at the appointment book entry you made in Taking Action on
page 30. Write it again on a sheet of paper. Put it in your portfolio.

Summing Up

I can:

☐ **1.** Read a memo from work.

☐ **2.** Read an appointment book.

☐ **3.** Scan for specific dates and times.

☐ **4.** Use It's to talk about time.

☐ **5.** Use an appointment book to organize information.

☐ **6.** _____

Money in Your Pocket

In this unit, you will:

1. Read about spending and saving money.
2. Read about shopping wisely.
3. Read and draw conclusions.
4. Understand **There is** and **There are.**
5. Use a chart to organize information.

 Accessing Information

Talk About It

What are the people doing? Why? What are they probably saying?

You Decide

Things are expensive these days. How can you save money when shopping? Companies use a lot of supplies. How can companies save money on supplies?

Key Vocabulary

A. In this unit, you will read about food and shopping. First, work with a partner. What do you like to eat? In your notebook, write a list.

B. Look at the pictures. Make a list of the food items. Then work with a partner. Take turns pointing at the words in your list and saying them aloud.

EXERCISE 1 Food
How much do they cost? Write prices on the lines.

1. spaghetti ___$.99___ a bag

2. coffee _____ a can

3. noodles _____ a box

4. chicken _____ a pound

5. grapes _____ a pound

Get the [Free] Great Values Card

Save money every day at Greatway!

Greatway has low, low everyday prices on all your favorite foods. And now you can save even more with the free Great Values Card—only from Greatway!

With the free Great Values Card, you get special savings on hundreds of sale items every week. Check our ad in the newspaper each Wednesday. Or get a copy of our ad at your store. Then you're ready to save, save, save!

The Great Values Card Is Free!

Just go to a Greatway Supermarket and fill out a form. You will get your free Great Values Card right away.

The Great Values Card is Easy!

You don't need coupons. Just bring your card with you. Show it to the cashier. The cash register will figure out your savings. Then see your savings on your receipt!

Greatway PRODUCE

Tomatoes
Great Values price
$.99
a pound
Regular price $1.49 a pound

Lettuce
Great Values special
Buy one, get one
FREE!
Regular price $1.29

Grapes
Great Values price
$.69
a pound
Regular price $1.79 a pound

EXERCISE 2 Answer the Questions

Write the answers in your notebook.

1. What do you get with a Great Values Card?

2. How much does a Great Values Card cost?

3. How much are grapes with a Great Values Card?

4. Mark doesn't have a Great Values Card. How much are grapes for Mark?

5. How do you get a Great Values Card?

Enriching Your Vocabulary

We use many expressions to talk about prices.

Expression	Meaning
$1.49 a pound	one pound costs $1.49
Buy one, get one free.	You buy one item at the regular price; you get a second one for nothing.
$1.39 each	one item costs $1.39
3 for $1.99	for $1.99 you get 3 items

EXERCISE 3 Prices

Look at the ad on page 34. Circle the expressions for prices.

Teamwork

Work with a partner. Student A looks at the Greatway ad on page 34. Student B looks at the Food Town ad on page 103. Complete the chart. Ask Student B about the prices at Food Town. If a food item is not on sale, write **Not on sale**. Then look at the information. Where do you want to shop? Discuss with your partner. Then share your answers with the class.

Food	Sale Price at Greatway	Sale Price at Food Town
Tomatoes	$.99	$1.19
Grapes		
Bananas		
Lettuce		

Giving Voice

Talk It Over

A. Everyone likes to save money. What are some ways to save money on food? Work with a small group. In your notebook, write a list.

B. Show your list to another group. Add the other group's ideas to your list. Then share your new list with the class. Use everyone's ideas to make a class list.

Look for discounts and special offers.

EXERCISE 4 How Much Are They?

Look at the ad. You have a Great Values Card. Answer the questions. Match. Write the letter on the line. There is one extra answer.

Grandmother's Soup

Buy one can get one can **FREE!**

Regular price $1.00 a can
Choose from chicken, tomato, and vegetable soup.

Gourmet Coffee

Great Values price **$7.00** a pound

Regular price $11.00 a pound.

Green Beans

Great Values price 3 cans for **$.99**

Regular price $.69 a can

Potatoes 5 pound bag

Great Values price **$1.50** a bag

Regular price $2.29

_____ **1.** a half pound of coffee

_____ **2.** a can of green beans

_____ **3.** four cans of soup

_____ **4.** two bags of potatoes

a. $0.33
b. $2.00
c. $3.00
d. $3.50
e. $4.00

Talk About It

great VALUES card Super Savings

132786

The Great Values Card can be used at all Greatway Supermarkets. Present this card at the checkout each time you shop. **This card is not transferable.**

Work with a group. List reasons for and against having a customer card. Answer these questions: Why do people have customer cards? What kind of information does the store get when you use a customer card? What are the advantages? What are the disadvantages?

READING STRATEGY
Read and Draw Conclusions

When you read, you often draw conclusions. A conclusion is something you figure out based on the information you have. For example, you are at the supermarket. You see that bread is on sale. You only have a little bread at home, and you eat sandwiches for lunch. So you conclude: It's a good idea to buy some bread on sale.

EXERCISE 5   Drawing Conclusions
Do you buy it? Write yes or **no** on the line.

_____ **1.** Lettuce is on sale at Greatway. The lettuce looks old.

_____ **2.** Your family drinks milk every day. Milk is on sale today. You have no milk at home.

_____ **3.** Usually, your son has trouble in school. This week he did great work. He loves chocolate. Chocolate is not on sale this week.

What does the restaurant serve?

Marco orders food for Little Italy restaurant. What do you think he needs to order? Read the menu.

Specials for Saturday

All-You-Can-Eat Spaghetti
Enjoy all the spaghetti you can eat. Choose spicy vegetable-tomato sauce or meat and tomato sauce. You also get salad, bread, and Italian cheese.
$7.95

Baked Italian Chicken
Enjoy our famous baked Italian chicken—fresh chicken baked with noodles in our own special tomato sauce. Start your meal with a fresh garden salad.
$8.95

Italian Chicken Salad
Lettuce and other fresh greens, topped with tomatoes, cheese, and chicken. Start with a bowl of soup.
$6.95

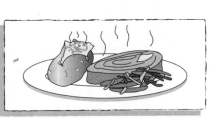

Fish
Delicious fish cooked in special Italian seasonings. Served with fresh vegetables and rice or baked potato. Start with a bowl of soup.
$8.95

Chocolate, Chocolate, Chocolate
Delicious chocolate cake with chocolate ice cream.
$3.95

We cook everything from fresh ingredients. 15% gratuity for parties of 6 or more. No substitutions. Baked potatoes after 5:00 PM only.

EXERCISE 6 Answer the Questions
Write the answers in your notebook.

1. How many specials are there today?

2. How much is the spaghetti?

3. What do customers get with the fish?

4. What do customers get with baked chicken?

5. Is the food fresh at the restaurant?

EXERCISE 7 Drawing Conclusions
Read the conclusions. Are the conclusions correct? Write **yes** or **no** on the line.

_____ 1. The fish is fresh.

_____ 2. The fish is more expensive than the chicken salad.

_____ 3. It's lunch time. Customers can get baked potatoes.

_____ 4. Lisa doesn't eat meat. She can't order spaghetti.

_____ 5. Paco can get vanilla ice cream with the cake.

LANGUAGE NOTE
There Is and There Are

We use **There is** and **There are** to talk about food.

There's a lot of chicken in the fridge. **There are** a lot of beans.

There is no spaghetti. **There are** no apples.

EXERCISE 8 There Is and There Are
Complete each sentence with **There is** or **There are**.

1. _____ no spaghetti.

2. _____ a lot of chicken.

3. _____ a few green beans.

4. _____ no ice cream.

STUDY SKILL
Healthful Snacks

It's nice to have a snack when you study. But choose a snack that's good for you. Fruit, crackers, and juice are good for you. Potato chips, soda, and candy are not very good for you.

Inventory

Chicken
    100 servings
Fish
    0 servings
Chocolate cake
    25 servings
Chocolate ice cream
    25 servings
Spaghetti
    500 servings

Taking Action

Ordering supplies is an important job. An inventory list is a list of a company's supplies. Look at the inventory list for Little Italy Italian Restaurant. Are there enough supplies? Talk about the list with your partner.

EXERCISE 9   Ordering Supplies

You work at Little Italy Italian Restaurant. The manager thinks that the restaurant will sell 150 servings of chicken, 50 servings of fish, 200 servings of spaghetti, and 90 servings of cake with ice cream. Look at the inventory list. How many servings should you order? Complete the form.

Rome Foods, Inc. Order Planning Sheet

Food	Number of Servings We Will Sell	Number of Servings in Stock	Number of Servings We Need
Chicken	150	100	50

 **Bridging to the Future**

Shopping lists are a good way to plan your shopping. Write a shopping list for one day in your notebook. Then work with a partner. What do you need? Tell your partner. What does your partner need? Tell the class.

Community Connection

Work with a small group. Your school is having money problems. There is very little money for supplies. Make a list of ways to get the supplies. Share your ideas with the class. Then make a class list.

Review

EXERCISE 10   Conclusions

Look at the menu description for a chicken sandwich. Then look at the supplies in the kitchen. What do you need to order? Check the boxes.

Italian Chicken Sandwich   **$4.95**

Enjoy out famous Italian chicken sandwich—fresh chicken and Italian cheese topped with lettuce, tomato, and onion on fresh Italian bread.

☐ chicken   ☐ tomatoes   ☐ Italian cheese

☐ Italian bread   ☐ lettuce   ☐ onions

Your Portfolio

In Talk It Over on page 36 you prepared a list of ways to save money. Look at your list again. Which 5 ideas do you want to try? Rewrite your list, and put it in your portfolio.

Summing Up

I can:

☐ **1.** Read about spending and saving money.

☐ **2.** Read about shopping wisely.

☐ **3.** Read and draw conclusions.

☐ **4.** Understand **There is** and **There are**.

☐ **5.** Use a chart to organize information.

☐ **6.** _____

Taking Care of Yourself

In this unit, you will:

1. Read about safety at work.
2. Read about safety at home.
3. Use pictures and captions to find the main idea.
4. Use commands.
5. Use a chart to organize numbers.

 ## Accessing Information

Talk About It
Where are the people? What are they doing? Why? Are the people staying safe?

You Decide
Why do people get hurt at work? At home? What can you do to stay safe?

Key Vocabulary

A. In this unit, you will read about staying safe at work and at home. First, work with a partner. In your notebook, write a list of words you know about staying safe.

B. Look at the picture. Take turns pointing to the words and saying them. Then talk about the picture. Is this a safe workplace? Why or why not?

1. run	6. safety gloves
2. slip	7. safety shoes
3. sign	8. hard hat
4. poison	9. hurt *or* injured
5. safety glasses	

EXERCISE 1   Make Rules
Work with a partner. In your notebook, write some safety rules for the workplace. Use the new vocabulary.

EXERCISE 2   Before You Read
Look at the pictures in the article on page 44. Answer the questions. Check the boxes.

1. What are the signs?

☐ safety signs   ☐ sale signs   ☐ street signs

2. What is the article probably about?

☐ safety at work   ☐ safety at home   ☐ safety in your car

How can you stay safe at work?

The Adventure Mountain Bicycle Company has an excellent safety record. How do the workers stay safe? Read the article.

A year ago, Adventure Mountain Bicycle Company had a big problem. There were many accidents and injuries. So the company made a safety plan. All the workers took a safety class. The workers all got new safety glasses and safety shoes. The company got new safety signs, too. And safety went up! On November 12, the company celebrated its success: no accidents or injuries for one year!

Adventure Mountain Bicycle Company
One year without an accident or injury

What Can You Do to Be Like the Workers at Adventure Mountain Bicycle Company?

To stay safe, follow these simple instructions.

1. Always wear your safety equipment. Many accidents happen because workers do not wear their safety equipment. Always wear safety glasses, gloves, safety shoes, and other equipment from your company.

2. Never run. Many accidents happen because employees run.

3. Read all safety signs at work. Ask a coworker or friend if you need help with the signs.

4. Accidents happen when people are tired, hungry, or sick. So get plenty of sleep before work. If you don't feel well, call in sick.

PLEASE work **SAFELY!**

5. Make sure equipment and machines are working correctly. If you notice a problem, tell your manager or a coworker right away.

If you follow these simple instructions, you can stay safe.

|||||||||||||||||||||||||||||||||||||||||||||||||||||||||||||

Workplace Accident Statistics

Every year millions of people in the U.S. are hurt on the job. Each day about 16 workers die from injuries at work and more than 17,000 are injured. The total cost is more than $121 billion a year.

|||||||||||||||||||||||||||||||||||||||||||||||||||||||||||||

EXERCISE 3 After You Read

Look at your answers to Exercise 2 on page 43. Were your answers correct?

EXERCISE 4 Charts

A. A chart is a good way to organize information. Complete this chart about accidents at work. Use the information in the article on page 44.

Problem	Number
workers hurt each day	
workers who die each day	
the cost of work-related injuries each year	

B. Look at the chart. Are accidents at work a problem in the U.S.? Explain your answer to your partner. Then share your partner's ideas with the class.

EXERCISE 5 Are They Staying Safe?

Look at the pictures. Are the workers staying safe? Write **yes** or **no**.

1. ___yes___   2. _____   3. _____

Enriching Your Vocabulary

Words such as **notice, warning, danger,** and **caution** are used on safety signs. Look at the signs on page 44. Circle the words that show danger.

Teamwork

Work with a partner. Student A looks at the safety instructions on page 44. Student B looks at the questions on page 104. Answer Student B's questions. Then switch roles and repeat the activity. Are your answers the same?

Giving Voice

Talk It Over

A. Every job has safety hazards. A safety hazard is something that is dangerous if you are not careful. For example, you can cut your hand inside a photocopier. Or you can burn your hand in a restaurant kitchen. Work with a partner. In your notebook, write a list of safety hazards at your workplace or a workplace you know about.

B. Share your list with another pair. What can you do to stay safe at work? Take turns giving each other advice. Use commands. Write down the advice in your notebook. Share the advice with the class.

LANGUAGE NOTE
Commands

The reading on safety at work uses commands. A command is a direct instruction. Understanding commands will help you improve your reading skills.

For affirmative commands, we use the verb with no subject.

    Put on your safety glasses!

For negative commands, we use **Don't** + verb.

    Don't run.

Look at the reading on page 44. Circle the commands.

EXERCISE 6   Make Rules

Look at the picture. Write two safety rules. Use commands.

1. _____

2. _____

Accessing Information

Talk About It

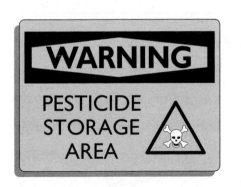

Pesticides kill insects. Pesticides are poisons. Poisons can make people sick or kill them. Work with a partner. Look at the sign and the product. Which one do you see at work? Which one do you see at home? What should people do when they see this sign and product? Where can you find other poisons at your workplace? At home?

> **READING STRATEGY**
> **Use Pictures and Captions to Find the Main Idea**
>
> Pictures and captions (the words under a picture) can often help you understand the meaning of what you read and help you find the main idea.

EXERCISE 7   Using Pictures and Captions

Look at the pictures and captions in the article on page 48. Circle the letter.

1. What is the main idea of the article?
   a. safety and health at work
   b. safety and health at home

2. The article is about
   a. avoiding bad food
   b. avoiding poisons

3. Which rule is probably in the article?
   a. Keep poisons away from children.
   b. Keep poisons out of your house.

TRACK 10

A terrible thing happened to Emma Rodriguez last year. Her little son, Edgar, drank some floor cleaner. She took him to the hospital. Edgar was OK. But Emma decided that she wanted to make her home safer.

Are Poisonings a Problem?

Yes. Accidental poisonings are a big danger in the United States, especially for children.

- In the United States, an accidental poisoning occurs about every 15 seconds. Half of them happen to children.
- Each year over 1,000,000 children in the U.S. are accidentally poisoned.
- Each year about 30 children die from accidental poisonings.
- Adults are affected, too. About 17 percent of accidental poisonings happen to people age 60 and older.
- About 90 percent of accidental poisonings happen at home.

What Things Are Poisonous?

Many common things are poisonous. Many home care products (like oven cleaner or bathroom cleaner) are poisonous. Medicine is poisonous if you take a lot of it. Even some holiday plants are poisonous.

Poinsettia and holly plants are poisonous.

Here are some ways to make your home safe.

Store Poisons Safely

Keep medicines and vitamins in places safe from children. Use a locked drawer or cabinet. Or put them on the top shelf of the medicine cabinet. Keep dangerous cleaning products out of reach of children. A good place is a locked cabinet or high shelf.

Use Products Safely

- Always read the instructions.
- Don't tell children that medicine is candy.

Don't keep cleaning supplies under the sink.
Children can find them.

- Always check the label before you take a medicine.
- Don't keep poisonous plants if you have children.

Get Help Right Away

If the poison is on the clothing or skin, take off the clothing and wash the skin. If the poison is in the eye, wash the eye. If the poison is in the air, get the person to fresh air. Then call the poison control center. Call 1-800-222-1222. This number will connect you to the poison control center for your city or state. If the person is not breathing, call 911.

EXERCISE 8   Using Pictures and Captions

Work with a partner. Review your answers to Exercise 7 on page 47.
Were your answers correct? Share your ideas with the class.

EXERCISE 9   Chart

A. As you know, a chart is a good way to organize information.
Complete this chart about accidental poisonings.

Problem	Number
children who are accidentally poisoned each year	
children who die from accidental poisonings each year	
percentage of accidental poisonings that are of adults over 60	
percentage of accidental poisonings at home	

B. Look at the chart. Are accidental poisonings a problem in the
U.S.? Why do they happen?

EXERCISE 10   Dangerous Products

Which of these products can be dangerous? Circle the letters.

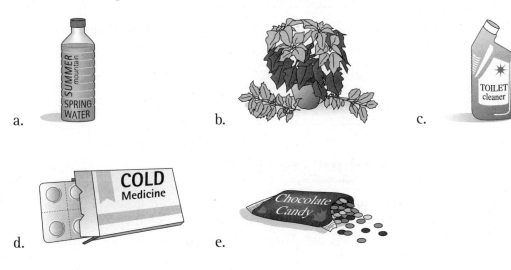

a. b. c.

d. e.

EXERCISE 11   Answer the Questions

Write your answers in your notebook.

1. Where should people keep medicine?

2. Where should people keep dangerous home care products?

3. What should people do if someone eats or drinks a dangerous
   product?

Taking Action

The people want to make their homes safe. Look at the list. Tell the people what to do.

1. Tim has a can of ant spray in his house. He keeps it under the sink. He has a young son. _____

_____

_____

2. Ana has a beautiful poinsettia plant. Ana's sister says that it's poisonous. Ana has a baby who is starting to walk.

_____

_____

_____

3. Ted keeps cleaning supplies under the sink in the bathroom. Sometimes he takes care of his sister's small children.

_____

_____

_____

4. Mrs. Green is 70 years old. She takes a lot of medicine. She keeps her medicine on the table next to her bed. Her grandchildren visit her every Sunday. _____

_____

_____

Bridging to the Future

You want to make your home safe. Work with a group. Make a list of things to check in your house. Share your list with the class. Make a class list. Then take your list home. Talk about it with your family.

Community Connection

Work with a group. Find out more information about the poison control center in your area. Use the phone book. Find the number for your poison control center. Find out what to do if a poisoning happens. Or use the Internet to find information.

Review

EXERCISE 12   Using Pictures and Captions

A. Look at the pictures and captions. What do you think the reading is about? Check the box.

☐   safety instructions for this product

☐   what to do if this product gets in your eye

☐   instructions for cleaning the bathroom

B. Write **yes** or **no** on the line.

___*no*___   **1.** This product is for cleaning kitchens.

_____   **2.** You can drink this product.

_____   **3.** You can keep this product under the sink if you have small children.

_____   **4.** You can clean the fridge with this product.

EXERCISE 13   Commands

Write commands. Use the product label.

1. _____ (use) this product in the bathroom.

2. _____ (use) this product in the kitchen.

3. _____ (keep) this product under the sink if you have small children.

GREATWAY
All-Purpose
Bathroom Cleanser

Use GREATWAY
All-Purpose Bathroom
Cleanser to keep your
bathroom clean.

☠ WARNING: POISON

Keep away from children. Do not use this product in the kitchen.

This product is for bathrooms only.

Your Portfolio

Review the unit. Find ways to stay safe at work. Write a list on a sheet of paper. Put the list in your portfolio.

Summing Up

I can:

☐ **1.** Read about safety at work.

☐ **2.** Read about safety at home.

☐ **3.** Use pictures and captions to find the main idea.

☐ **4.** Use commands.

☐ **5.** Use a chart to organize numbers.

☐ **6.** _____

Tools and Technology

In this unit, you will:

1. Read about telephone features.
2. Read about using a machine at work.
3. Use background information to help you read.
4. Make comparisons with adjectives and **–er/more**.
5. Use a KWL chart to help you read.

 Accessing Information

Talk About It
What are the people doing?
What machines are they using?
What machines do you use?

You Decide
What machines do you use at home? At work?

Key Vocabulary

In this unit, you will read about everyday machines—telephones and vacuum cleaners. Here are some words we often use when talking about these machines.

ring—the noise a phone makes when it gets a call

miss a call—not get a call

message—You call a person. The person doesn't answer the phone. So you leave your name and telephone number.

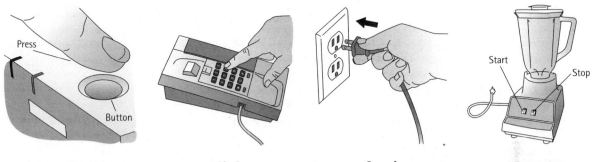

press, button   **dial**   **plug in**   **start, stop**

EXERCISE 1   Vocabulary

Look at the words above. Are they for phones or vacuum cleaners or both? In your notebook, write 3 lists: *phone only, vacuum only,* and *phone and vacuum.* Add more words you use with machines.

EXERCISE 2   Before You Read

A KWL chart helps you read. (K means "know," W means "want to know," and L means "learned.") In a KWL chart, you write what you **know** and what you **want** to know. Then you read. After you read, you write what you **learned**. The reading on the next page is about special features of telephones. Copy the KWL chart in your notebook. Complete the K and W columns of the KWL chart about special features of telephones.

K	W	L
What I **know** about special features of telephones	What I **want** to know about special features of telephones	What I **learned** about special features of telephones

Do you need caller ID?

Southeastern Bell Telephone has new phone features

Voice Mail You're not home. With voice mail, callers can leave messages. You can listen to your messages at home. You can get your messages from any other phone, too.

Call Waiting You're on the phone. With call waiting, your phone makes a special beep when you get another call. Then you can answer the call. You don't need to hang up on the other call. You can switch from call to call.

Talking Call Waiting Talking call waiting is the same as call waiting. But with talking call waiting, your phone tells you the name and number of the caller. Talking call waiting is available in English and Spanish.

Call Forwarding With call forwarding, you send all of your phone calls to another number. You can send your calls to your cell phone or to any other phone.

These **special features** make your life easier!

Repeat Calling Don't let a busy signal stop you! With repeat calling, your phone will keep calling a busy number. Then the phone will call you.

Caller ID With Caller ID, you can see the name and number of callers. This way, you answer only the calls you want.

Voice Dialing With voice dialing, you say the name of the person you want to call. The phone calls that number.

Three-Way Calling Do you ever want to talk to your brother and your sister together? Now you can. With three-way calling, you can talk to two people at the same time.

Second Phone Line Get a second phone line for your children. Or use it for your computer or fax machine.

Rates and Services

Voice Mail	$9.95 a month
Call Waiting	$2.25 a month
Talking Call Waiting	$2.50 a month
Call Forwarding	$2.25 a month
Repeat Calling	$2.25 a month
Caller ID	$5.95 a month
Voice Dialing	$3.95 a month
Three-Way Calling	$3.95 a month
Second Phone Line	$9.00 a month

EXERCISE 3   After You Read

A. Look at the KWL chart you prepared on page 53. What did you learn about phone features from the reading? Write some notes in the L column of the chart.

B. Did the KWL chart help you read the reading? Tell your partner. What did your partner say? Tell the class.

EXERCISE 4   Match

Which feature do you need? Write the letter on the line.

_____ 1. A lot of salespeople call you. You want to know who is calling before you answer the phone.

_____ 2. Your children talk on the phone a lot. You want to use the phone for your new computer.

_____ 3. Your hand is injured. It's hard to dial the phone with your hand.

_____ 4. When you are at work, you get a lot of phone calls at home. You want to get messages from the callers.

_____ 5. You are away from home a lot. You want to get your calls on your cell phone.

_____ 6. You talk on the phone a lot. You get calls when you are on the phone. You don't want to miss calls.

_____ 7. Your mother lives with you. She wants call waiting, but she can't read the caller ID screen.

_____ 8. You call your sister alot, but you often get a busy signal. You want to talk to her as soon as she is finished with her call.

a. voice mail
b. call waiting
c. talking call waiting
d. call forwarding
e. repeat calling
f. caller ID
g. voice dialing
h. second phone line

Teamwork

Work with a partner. Student A looks at the rates and services on page 54. Student B looks at the questions on page 104. Answer Student B's questions. Then switch roles and repeat the activity. Are your answers the same?

Giving Voice

Talk It Over

A. Review your answers to Teamwork on pages 55 and 104. The phone company has a special offer on phone features. Read about the special offer. Which people in Teamwork should get the special offer? Why?

Do you use your phone a lot?
Do you want special features at a special price?

Southeastern Bell
The Phone Lover's Special

SPECIAL!

You Get:
Caller ID
Voice Mail
Voice Dialing
Call Forwarding

$12.95

B. What features do you want? Make a list. How much will the features cost? $_____ Should you get the Phone Lover's Special? Why or why not? Tell your group.

Enriching Your Vocabulary

Telephones make sounds. What are the names of the sounds?

Sound	When You Hear It
dial tone	Your phone is ready for you to dial.
busy signal	You call a person, but the person is already on the phone.
ring	You are getting a call.
beep	You have call waiting. You are on the phone and you get another call.

EXERCISE 5   Telephone Sounds
You hear the sound. What do you do? Match.

___d___ **1.** beep

_____ **2.** busy signal

_____ **3.** ring

_____ **4.** dial tone

a. answer the phone
b. hang up and call again later
c. dial a phone number
d. use call waiting to answer the call

Accessing Information

Talk About It

You just got some new phone features. What features did you get?
Which features are most important to you? Why? Tell your partner.
Then make a list of three important features and three features that
are not important to you. Share your lists with the class.

READING STRATEGY
Use Background Information to Help You Read

When you read, your background information helps you understand the reading.
Use your background information to help you read the reading on the next page
about a new automatic vacuum cleaner.

EXERCISE 6   Use a KWL Chart

What do you know about automatic vacuum cleaners? What do
you want to know? Copy the KWL chart in your notebook. Then
complete the K and W columns of the chart.

K	W	L
What I **know** about automatic vacuum cleaners	What I **want** to know about automatic vacuum cleaners	What I **learned** about automatic vacuum cleaners

Are you tired of vacuuming floors?

Workers at the Southtown Convention Center and Hotel spend a lot of time vacuuming. This week they are testing an automatic vacuum cleaner. Read about the automatic vacuum cleaner.

Intelligent Systems Automatic Vacuum

Press three buttons, and this new automatic vacuum cleaner will clean the floor in a room in 10 minutes.

This small, powerful vacuum will move around the room and clean the carpet. You are free to clean the bathroom and make the bed.

The automatic vacuum cleaner is **faster** than a regular vacuum cleaner. The automatic vacuum cleaner is **easier** than a regular vacuum cleaner, too.

This new automatic vacuum cleaner moves in a circle. When it touches furniture or a wall, it changes direction. When the carpet is clean, the vacuum cleaner stops.

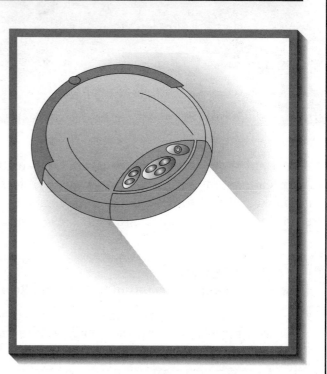

To use the new automatic vacuum cleaner, follow these instructions:

1. Pick up clothes, toys, and other things from the floor.

2. Put the automatic vacuum cleaner in the middle of the room.

3. Select the size of the room. Press **small, medium,** or **large.**

4. Select the type of carpeting. Press **thin** or **thick.**

5. Press the **on** button. Then you can clean the bathroom, make the bed, etc.

6. The vacuum cleaner stops automatically when the carpet is clean. You can press the **off** button to stop it, too.

7. After you clean a room, empty the vacuum cleaner. Hold the vacuum cleaner over a trash can. Then open the door.

The automatic vacuum cleaner uses a special battery. You need to charge the battery every night. Plug in the vacuum cleaner at the end of the day. The vacuum cleaner will be ready to use again the next day.

EXERCISE 7   Using Background Information

A. Look at the KWL chart you prepared on page 57. What did you learn about automatic vacuum cleaners from the reading? Write some notes in the L column of the chart.

B. Did the KWL chart help you when you read the reading? Tell your partner. What did your partner say? Tell the class.

EXERCISE 8   What Do You Do?

You work at Southtown Convention Center and Hotel. You are starting work. You want to use the automatic vacuum cleaner. What do you do? Write numbers from 1 to 8.

_____ a. Empty the vacuum cleaner.

_____ b. Plug in the vacuum cleaner and charge the battery for tomorrow.

_____ c. Press **thin** or **thick**.

_____ d. Put the vacuum cleaner in the middle of the room.

_____ e. Put clothes, toys, etc., in the closet.

_____ f. The vacuum cleaner cleans the room. You do other work.

_____ g. Press the **on** button.

_____ h. Press **small**, **medium**, or **large**.

LANGUAGE NOTE
Adjectives and –er/more

The reading on the automatic vacuum cleaner uses adjectives and **-er/more**. Understanding adjectives and **–er/more** will help you improve your reading skills.

To compare two things using adjectives, we use **-er** or **more**. Look at the examples.

An automatic vacuum cleaner is **faster** than a regular vacuum cleaner.

An automatic vacuum cleaner is **more** expensive than a regular vacuum cleaner.

Good is irregular. Use **better** to compare things:

An automatic vacuum cleaner is **better** than a regular vacuum cleaner.

STUDY SKILL
Use a Computer

A computer is a tool that can help you with work and school. You can use a computer to type papers. You can use a computer to send e-mail. You can use a computer to find information on the Internet. You can buy things on the Internet, too.

EXERCISE 9   Comparing Vacuum Cleaners

Work with a partner. Take turns comparing a regular vacuum cleaner with an automatic vacuum cleaner. Use **–er** or **more**. Use these adjectives: large, small, cheap, expensive, heavy.

Taking Action

fax machine

A. What machines do you use at your job? Make a list.

B. Work with a partner. Ask your partner to choose one of your machines. Tell your partner how to use the machine. Then ask your partner for directions for one of his or her machines.

EXERCISE 10 Directions

Bring in directions for a simple machine in your home, such as a coffeemaker or an iron. Work with a small group. Take turns talking about your directions. Tell your group the name of the machine. Tell them how to use the machine.

EXERCISE 11 Should You Buy It?

Does the automatic vacuum cleaner really work? A reporter for the city newspaper tested the vacuum cleaner. Here are the results.

Kind of floor	Results
Thin carpeting	Excellent
Thick carpeting	Terrible
Wood floors	Good
Kitchen floors	Terrible
Stairs with carpeting	Terrible

Should people buy the automatic vacuum cleaner? Talk over your ideas with a group. Share your ideas with the class.

Bridging to the Future

I want to use computers . . .

to send e-mail

Work with a partner. What do you want to use computers for? Make a list.

Community Connection

Go to the public library. Make a list of the machines people can use there. Ask a librarian for help if you don't know the names of the machines. Find out how to use one of the machines. Write directions or bring a copy of the directions to class.

Review

EXERCISE 12   Using Background Information

A. The paragraph gives instructions for a cell phone. Write a KWL chart in your notebook. Follow the example on page 53. Complete the K and W columns.

B. Read the paragraph. Complete the L column of the KWL chart. Then check the boxes.

☐ The KWL chart helped me use background information I know about cell phones.

☐ The KWL chart helped me read the paragraph faster.

☐ The KWL chart helped me understand the paragraph better.

Your New 4250i Cell Phone from A-1 Communications

Using Your New Phone

First turn on your cell phone. Press the red ON/OFF button. The phone will turn on. To make a call, press DIAL. Then press 1, the area code, and the telephone number. To end the call, press END. When you are not using the phone, turn it off. Press the red ON/OFF button.

Your Portfolio

Use the information you shared in Taking Action on page 60 to write a few simple directions on how to use the machine. Put the instructions in your portfolio.

Summing Up
I can:

☐ 1. Read about telephone features.

☐ 2. Read about using a machine at work.

☐ 3. Use background information to help me read.

☐ 4. Make comparisons with adjectives and –er/more.

☐ 5. Use a KWL chart to help me read.

☐ 6. _____

Our History

In this unit, you will:

1. Read about murals.
2. Read about famous immigrants to the United States.
3. Use related words to help you read.
4. Understand the past tense of **be.**
5. Use a Venn diagram to organize information.

Accessing Information

Talk About It
Where are the people? What are they doing?

You Decide
This unit is about our past. Is the past important? Why do you think so?

Key Vocabulary

A. In this unit, we are going to read about history. First, we will read about large paintings called murals. These paintings show important things from history. Then we will read about famous immigrants to the U.S. Immigrants are people who move to the U.S. from another country. Work with a partner. What do you know about U.S. history? Write a list in your notebook.

Abraham
Lincoln

B. Study the vocabulary.

politician

congresswoman/congressman

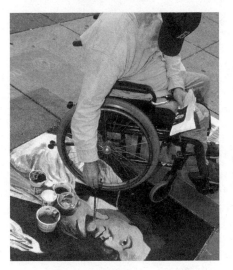

artist

musician

EXERCISE 1   Vocabulary

Write the name of a politician, congressman or congresswoman, artist, and musician that you know.

politician	congressman	artist	musician

Why do people paint murals?

Murals Tell Our History

A mural is a large painting. Usually, murals are in places where everyone can see them. Murals are often in schools and post offices. They are also on the sides of buildings. Murals make cities more beautiful. Murals also teach us about our history. Many cities in the U.S. have beautiful murals. Here are the stories of two murals in Chicago.

Fredric Chopin Mural, Chopin School

Florian Durzynski painted this mural in the 1930s. It shows the famous Polish musician Fredric Chopin. Chopin lived from 1810 to 1849, and he wrote a lot of beautiful piano music. The mural shows scenes from Poland. It also shows dancers. Some dancers are wearing traditional Polish clothes. Other dancers are wearing ballet clothes. This is because Chopin wrote traditional Polish music and ballet music.

Mexican people have made a lot of murals in Chicago. Murals are very popular in Mexico. In the 1960s, many Mexicans began to come to Chicago. They made murals in their new city. Now Chicago has about 300 murals by Mexican artists.

Heroes of Mexico Mural, Orozco Academy

This large mural was made by students at Orozco Academy in Chicago. This part of the mural shows a famous Mexican artist, Frida Kahlo. Frida Kahlo was born in 1907 and died in 1954. She painted many beautiful paintings. Many of her paintings had traditional Mexican subjects. Her paintings are in museums all over the world. Now Mexican children in Chicago can look at this mural and feel proud of their history.

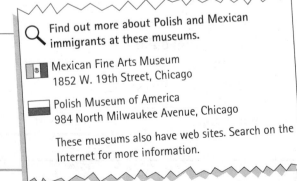

Find out more about Polish and Mexican immigrants at these museums.

Mexican Fine Arts Museum
1852 W. 19th Street, Chicago

Polish Museum of America
984 North Milwaukee Avenue, Chicago

These museums also have web sites. Search on the Internet for more information.

EXERCISE 2   Answer the Questions

1. What is a mural?

2. Where is the Chopin mural?

3. Where is the Kahlo mural?

4. Why is Chopin important?

5. Why is Kahlo important?

EXERCISE 3   Venn Diagram

A. A Venn diagram helps us compare and contrast. Look at the Venn diagram about Chopin and Kahlo. Fill in the circle on the left with information about Chopin. Fill in the circle on the right with information about Kahlo. Fill in the gray area in the middle with information about both of them. Read the information in the list below. Write the number in the correct place. For example, the number 1 is in the gray area in the middle because both Chopin and Kahlo are shown in a mural.

1. shown in a mural

2. lived in the 1800s

3. lived in the 1900s

4. from Europe

5. from Mexico

6. wrote music

7. famous

8. wrote ballets

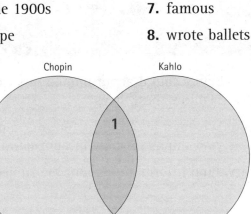

Chopin   Kahlo

1

B. Use the information to write sentences about Chopin and Kahlo. Write your sentences in your notebook. Share your sentences with the class.

Teamwork

Work with a partner. Student A looks at the museum information on page 64. Student B looks at the questions on page 105. Answer Student B's questions. Then switch roles. Are your answers the same?

Talk It Over

Are there any murals in your community? Where? What do they show? Talk over your answers with a group. Share your group's answers with the class.

EXERCISE 4   Making a Mural

Work with a group. Plan a mural about immigrants from your country or countries. Follow these steps.

1. In your notebook, create a list of ideas for your mural. Think of people, places, and things to show in your mural.

2. Go to the library. Find information about the subject of your mural.

3. In your group, create a simple drawing for your mural. Then write a few sentences in your notebook about your drawing.

4. Share your drawing and your sentences with the class.

5. If possible, use everyone's ideas to create a class mural.

STUDY SKILL
Use an
Encyclopedia

When you need information, you can check many different books. One great source of information is an encyclopedia. An encyclopedia contains articles on many different subjects. Today, many encyclopedias are on CD-ROM and the Internet, but they are also in books. Go to the library and use the encyclopedia to find information for your mural.

Accessing Information

Talk About It

A group of high school students created this mural. It's in a famous museum, the Oriental Institute in Chicago. Look at the mural. What does it show? Why are murals important?

Enriching Your Vocabulary

Look at the list of countries and nationalities.

Country	Nationality
China	Chinese
Mexico	Mexican
Morocco	Moroccan

Circle the countries and nationalities in the reading on page 64.

EXERCISE 5   Countries and Nationalities
In your notebook, write sentences about the country and nationality of three students.

READING STRATEGY
Use Related Words To Help You Read

When you read, you will see related words. For example, **Mexico** and **Mexican** are related. **Mexico** is the name of a country. **Mexican** describes people or things from Mexico. Seeing related words helps you increase your vocabulary. As you read the article on the next page, try to find a word related to **Italy**.

Ingrid is from Poland. She's Polish.

How have immigrants helped their new country?

Many immigrants come to their new country to find work. Sometimes, immigrants use their work to help other immigrants. What did they do? Read the article.

TRACK 14

Immigrants play an important role in the history of the United States. Here are the stories of 3 immigrants and children of immigrants.

Fiorello LaGuardia was the son of immigrants from Italy. His family did not have a lot of money. He was a lawyer and a politician. He helped immigrants with legal problems. LaGuardia was the first Italian American in the U.S. Congress. At this time, women could not vote. So the young congressman helped women get the right to vote. Many children of immigrants worked. So they didn't go to school. LaGuardia helped make a law for all children to go to school. In 1933, he became mayor of New York City. He helped poor people. The city built apartments for people. He also helped find jobs for people.

Fiorello LaGuardia

Cesar Chavez

Cesar Chavez was the grandson of an immigrant from Mexico. His family was very poor. They were farm workers. The work was hard and dangerous. Because he was poor, he could not go to school. Chavez wanted to help farm workers. He decided to start a union. Many farm workers joined the union. Chavez helped farm workers get better pay. He also made sure children of farm workers could go to school. In 1991, he got an important prize: the Aztec Eagle, from the government of Mexico. After his death in 1993, he won the U.S. Presidential Medal of Honor.

Stefania Chmielinska was an immigrant from Poland. She was a seamstress. She worked hard, but she didn't make a lot of money. She wanted women to vote. She wanted women to go to college. In 1899, she started the Polish Women's Alliance of America. This organization helped Polish families in the U.S. This organization helped immigrants go to high school and college. It started a newspaper in Polish. It helped immigrants find houses and jobs. Stefania Chmielinska won an important prize from the Polish government: The Gold Cross of Service.

Stefania Chmielinska

EXERCISE 6   Related Words

A. What word related to Italy did you find? What does it mean?

_____

B. Find more related words. First, circle **law** and **Congress** in the reading. Then circle the related words.

EXERCISE 7   Who Was It?

Check the box or boxes.

	LaGuardia	Chavez	Chmielinska
1. His or her family was from Mexico.	☐	☐	☐
2. His or her family was from Italy.	☐	☐	☐
3. His or her family was from Poland.	☐	☐	☐
4. He or she won prizes.	☐	☐	☐
5. He or she helped people go to school.	☐	☐	☐
6. He or she helped people get jobs.	☐	☐	☐
7. He or she helped women get to vote.	☐	☐	☐
8. He or she started organizations.	☐	☐	☐
9. He or she was a politician.	☐	☐	☐
10. He or she helped people find places to live.	☐	☐	☐
11. He or she started a newspaper.	☐	☐	☐
12. He or she was an immigrant.	☐	☐	☐
13. His or her mother and father were immigrants.	☐	☐	☐
14. His or her grandfather was an immigrant.	☐	☐	☐
15. He or she was poor.	☐	☐	☐

EXERCISE 8   Venn Diagram

Complete the diagram. Write numbers from Exercise 7 in the correct place.

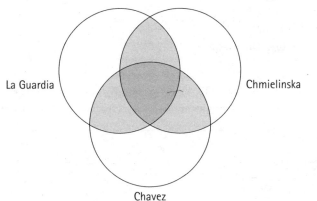

La Guardia

Chmielinska

Chavez

Taking Action

A. LaGuardia, Chavez, and Chmielinska helped immigrants with their problems. What problems do immigrants have today? Make a list in your notebook.

B. What organizations can help you with your problems? Use the phone book and the Internet to find community groups that can help with the problems. In your notebook, write the name, address, and phone number of each organization. Then write a few words about the problems that the group can help with.

They need good jobs.

Bridging to the Future

Work with a group. You want to help people who are new to the country. What can you do? In your notebook, write a few ideas. Share your ideas with the class.

Family Connection

Choose one of the leaders: LaGuardia, Chavez, or Chmielinska. Talk to your family or friends about the person. Is the person a good leader? Why? Ask your family or friends to name other leaders who help immigrants. Share your ideas with the class.

LANGUAGE NOTE
Past Tense of *Be*

The reading on famous immigrants uses the past tense of **be**. Understanding the past tense of **be** will help you improve your reading skills.

The past tenses of the verb **be** (**am, is, are**) are **was** and **were**. Look at the examples.

I
He, She } **was** from Mexico.

You
We } **were** from Mexico.
They

Look at the reading on page 68. Circle the examples of **was** and **were**. Then, in your notebook, write two sentences about one of the people. Use **was** and **were**.

Review

EXERCISE 9   Patsy Mink

A. Read the article about Patsy Mink. Then compare and contrast Patsy Mink and Cesar Chavez.

	Mink	Chavez
1. He or she was a politician.	☐	☐
2. He or she helped people.	☐	☐
3. He or she started a union.	☐	☐
4. He or she helped Asians.	☐	☐
5. He or she helped Hispanics.	☐	☐
6. He or she helped people go to school.	☐	☐

B. Use the information from A to make a Venn diagram in your notebook. Follow the example on page 65.

EXERCISE 10   Related Words

Look at the reading on Patsy Mink. Find words related to **Japan** and **Congress**. Write them in your notebook.

Your Portfolio

Review the information you gathered in Taking Action on page 70. Put the information in your portfolio.

Summing Up

I can:

☐ **1.** Read about murals.

☐ **2.** Read about famous immigrants to the United States.

☐ **3.** Use related words to help me read.

☐ **4.** Understand the past tense of **be**.

☐ **5.** Use a Venn diagram to organize information.

☐ **6.** _____

Patsy Mink

Hawaii Congresswoman

Patsy Mink was a congresswoman from Hawaii. Her grandparents were Japanese immigrants. They moved from Japan to Hawaii in the 1880s. Patsy Mink was born in 1928. She was a good student. She wanted to be a doctor, but it was difficult for women to go to medical school at that time. So she became a lawyer. In 1965, she became a congresswoman. In Congress, she helped Asian Americans and women. She also worked hard to help people go to school. She died in 2002.

Home Sweet Home

In this unit, you will:

1. Read about homes and apartments.
2. Read about services in your community.
3. Scan for specific information.
4. Understand the simple present tense.
5. Use a T-chart to organize information.

 Accessing Information

Talk About It

What are the people doing? Why? What information are they looking for?

You Decide

Why do people move? How do you find a new house or apartment? Is the neighborhood good? How do you know?

Key Vocabulary

A. In this unit, you will read about homes and neighborhoods. First, work with a partner. In your notebook, write a list of words you know about homes and neighborhoods.

B. Look at the picture. Find the words on your list. Then work with your partner. Take turns pointing at the places and saying the words aloud.

EXERCISE 1   In Your Neighborhood

A. Which places are in your neighborhood? Which ones do you use? Check the boxes.

	I use it.	It's in my neighborhood.
1. supermarket	☐	☐
2. post office	☐	☐
3. school	☐	☐
4. library	☐	☐
5. bus stop	☐	☐
6. park	☐	☐
7. mall	☐	☐
8. health center	☐	☐
9. _____	☐	☐
10. _____	☐	☐

B. Work with a partner. Which services do you use? Tell your partner. What services does your partner use? Listen to your partner. Then tell the class.

EXERCISE 2 Before You Read

Find the information in the brochure and ad.

1. Where are the apartments? _____

2. Is there cable TV? _____

3. How much is the rent for a two-bedroom apartment? _____

Where can you find a great apartment?

Martin and Maria Melendez are expecting a new baby girl. They have two sons now so they need a larger apartment. They saw an ad for Parkview Apartments. They went to the apartments and got this brochure.

TRACK 15

Parkview Apartments

Parkview offers nice apartments in a beautiful setting.

Parkview Apartments are at Main Street and Park Avenue in Lake City. The apartments are large and new. The apartments have one, two, or three bedrooms and one or two bathrooms.

Special Features

- Each building has a laundry room.
- There is a playground for children.
- A school is nearby.
- Each apartment has free parking for two cars. A bus stop is nearby.
- Parkview Apartments are close to a supermarket, a mall, a bank, and a post office.
- Cable TV and heat are free.

living room

bedroom

kitchen

bathroom

FOR RENT

Parkview Apartments 2 bdrm, 1 bath apts in nice bldg. Nr. supermarket and a school. Free pkg, heat, and cable. Rent: $500, deposit: $500. Call Ms. Green, (916) 555-7000. **Special offer:** Rent an apartment in August and get a free microwave oven in your apartment.

EXERCISE 3   After You Read

Work with a partner. Answer the questions.

1. Look at your answers to Exercise 2 on page 74. Were your answers correct?

2. Do Martin and Maria Melendez want to live at Parkview Apartments? What do you think? Why or why not?

EXERCISE 4   Yes or No

Write **yes** or **no** on the line.

_____no_____ 1. People buy apartments at Parkview Apartments.

_____ 2. Parkview has laundry rooms.

_____ 3. Parkview has no parking.

_____ 4. You can get a four-bedroom apartment.

_____ 5. Heat is free.

_____ 6. Parkview is a good place for families with children.

EXERCISE 5   T–Charts

A. T-chart is a way to organize information into two groups. For example, you want to rent an apartment, but you are not sure if the apartment is good for you. Make a chart with two columns: *Good* and *Not Good*. Then organize the information in two columns. Look at the example.

Good	Not Good
Low rent	Far from schools
Quiet	Not near a bus stop

Now you can use the information to help you make a decision.

B. Help Maria and Martin. They need a two-bedroom apartment that's good for their 2 sons. They do a lot of laundry, and they go to the supermarket every day. They use a bank near their jobs. They can spend $600 a month for rent. They need parking for 3 cars. In your notebook, make a T-chart about Parkview Apartments for Maria and Martin. Follow the example.

Teamwork

Work with a partner. Student A looks at the apartment ad on page 74. Student B looks at the questions on page 105. Answer Student B's questions. Then switch roles. Compare your answers.

Giving Voice

Talk It Over

A. Think about your apartment. Is it large? Small? Old? New? How many rooms does it have? Write a few words in your notebook.

B. Work with a partner. Look at your notes. Tell your partner about your home. What's your partner's house or apartment like? Tell the class.

EXERCISE 6   Your Apartment

A. You need a new apartment. What's most important to you? Make a T-chart. Follow the example on page 75.

2 or more bedrooms   free cable TV
large kitchen   near schools
many closets   lots of parking
laundry in the building   near a bus stop
good neighborhood   low rent

Important	Not Important

B. Share your T-chart with your partner. What's important to you? Why? Tell your partner. What's important to your partner? Tell the class.

Enriching Your Vocabulary

An abbreviation is a short form of a word. Usually, an abbreviation has a period at the end. Apartment ads have many abbreviations. Look at the T-chart.

Word	Abbreviation
large	lg.
small	sm.

Look at the ad on page 74. Circle the abbreviations. Then look at the brochure. Circle the words for the abbreviations. Use the words to make a T-chart of words and abbreviations in your notebook.

Accessing Information

Talk About It

What do the pictures and words tell you about Parkview Apartments? Do you think many people want to live at Parkview Apartments? Why or why not?

> **READING STRATEGY**
> **Scan for Specific Information**
>
> As you know, when you read you sometimes want to find specific information, such as a price, a phone number, or an address. You don't read every word. You only look for the information. This skill is called **scanning**.

EXERCISE 7   Scanning

A. When do you scan? Check the boxes.

☐ **1.** You want to find out the price of an apartment.

☐ **2.** You want to read an article about your town.

☐ **3.** You want to know the number of bedrooms in an apartment.

☐ **4.** You need to know the address of an apartment building.

☐ **5.** You have a storybook and want to read it to your children.

B. What's the phone number of Parkview Apartments? Scan the apartment ad. _____

EXERCISE 8   Scan the Article

Scan the article on the next page. What is the address of Wall's Supermarket? Write it on the line. _____

What makes your neighborhood nice?

Martin and Maria Melendez want to live in a nice neighborhood. They have a brochure about the Parkview neighborhood.

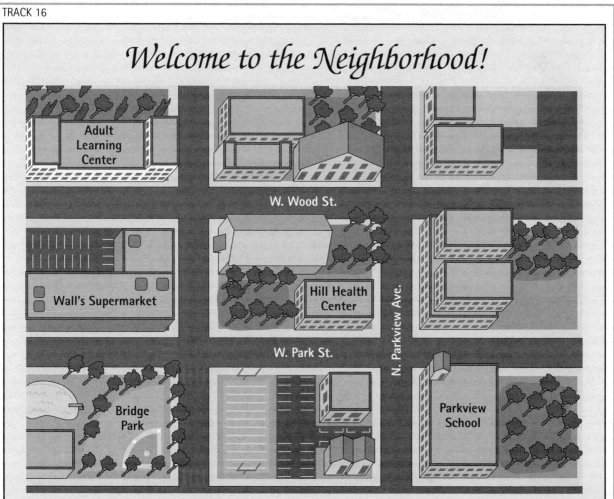

Welcome to the Neighborhood!

Adult Learning Center

W. Wood St.

Wall's Supermarket

Hill Health Center

N. Parkview Ave.

W. Park St.

Bridge Park

Parkview School

The Parkview Neighborhood has many community services.

West Wood Street Adult Learning Center
103 W. Wood St.
(916) 555-6789
This learning center offers English classes for adults. It offers high school classes, too.

Wall's Supermarket
310 W. Park St.
(916) 555-2700
Wall's is open 24 hours a day, 7 days a week.

Parkview School
3010 N. Parkview Ave.
Call (916) 555-5600 for information.

Hill Health Center
230 W. Park St.
(916) 555-1000

Community Services
The Parkview Neighborhood has 3 banks and a post office.

Transportation
Five bus lines stop in the Parkview Neighborhood. Buses go downtown and to schools.

Bridge Park
We have fields for baseball, football, and soccer. The Senior Center has activities for adults age 60 and older. We have 15 classes for children, including swimming, photography, sewing, and more!

EXERCISE 9   Scanning
Scan the reading on page 78. Answer the questions.

1. How many banks are in the neighborhood? _____

2. What's the phone number of Hill Health Center? _____

3. Can adults study photography at the park? _____

4. Can you take a bus to the airport? _____

5. It's 6:00 Sunday morning. Is Wall's Supermarket open? _____

EXERCISE 10   How's the Neighborhood?
Work with a partner. Read the list of services. Which ones are
in the Parkview neighborhood? Which ones aren't in the
neighborhood? Write a T-chart in your notebook. Follow the
example below.

supermarket	post office	school	library
bus stop	park	mall	senior center
bank	health center	gas station	adult learning center

In the Neighborhood	Not in the Neighborhood
supermarket	mall

EXERCISE 11   Help the People
Read about the people. Where should they go?
Write the place from Exercise 10 on the line.

1. Mary Jane wants to read a book.

   _____

2. Mr. Wells needs to see a doctor.

   _____

3. Ms. Espinoza is 70 years old. She
   wants to make new friends.

   _____

4. Tim needs to buy milk, bread,
   and juice.

   _____

5. Mr. Delgado wants to learn English.

   _____

> **LANGUAGE NOTE**
> **Simple Present Tense**
>
> The reading on the Parkview Neighborhood uses the
> simple present tense. We use the simple present tense to
> talk about things that are always true. Understanding
> the simple present tense will help you improve your
> reading skills.
>
> | I | offer | have |
> |---|---|---|
> | you | offer | have |
> | he, she, it | offers | has |
> | we | offer | have |
> | they | offer | have |
>
> The Adult Learning Center **offers** English classes.
>
> The park **has** classes for children.
>
> Look at the reading again. Circle the verbs in the
> simple present tense.

Taking Action

A. You want to find a good neighborhood. What's important to you? What's not important to you? In your notebook, write a T-chart. Follow the example on page 75.

bank	library
post office	supermarket
school	mall
park	adult education center
health center	bus stop

B. Take your list home. Discuss it with your family. Add more places.

C. Work with a group. Read your lists to the class. Listen to the other learners. Then talk about places you can live.

Bridging to the Future

A. You want a new apartment. What questions do you ask the apartment manager? Work with a partner. Write 2 or 3 questions. Use your answers to Taking Action to help you.

B. Work with a partner. One student is looking for an apartment. The other student is the apartment manager. Take turns asking and answering questions. Use the model.

A: How many bedrooms do you need?

B: Two. Is heat free?

A: Yes, it is.

Workplace Connection

Work with a group to solve this problem.

Luis has a good job at AB Electronics. His pay is good. He has a good boss, too. AB Electronics is near Luis's house. He doesn't have a car. He always walks to work. But the company is moving to another part of the city next month. Luis will be far from his job.

Help Luis. What can Luis do? Talk over your ideas. Then share your ideas with the class. Use everyone's ideas to create a class idea list.

Review

EXERCISE 12   Scanning

Sometimes, you see a For Rent sign on a building. Scan the For Rent sign. Answer the questions.

1. How much is the rent? _____

2. How many bedrooms does
   the apartment have? _____

APARTMENT **FOR RENT**

For Rent in this Building
Lg. 2 bedroom apartment with 1 bath. Many lg. clsts. sm. ktch. Nr. a park, post office, sch., bus stop. Free pkg. for 2 cars. Rent: $750 a month
(414) 555-5025

EXERCISE 13   Finding an Apartment

Should the people rent the apartment?
Write yes or **no**.

_____ 1. Carlos likes to run in the park.

_____ 2. Yumi works at the mall. She wants to live near her job.

_____ 3. Boris wants to be on a bus line.

_____ 4. Tom can only pay $500 a month in rent.

_____ 5. Mr. and Mrs. Choi need free parking for two cars.

Your Portfolio

Work with a group. Look at the list of words and abbreviations you made in Enriching Your Vocabulary. Create a group list. Then find an apartment ad that has some of the abbreviations. Circle the abbreviations. Put the list and ad in your portfolio.

Summing Up

I can:

☐ 1. Read about homes and apartments.

☐ 2. Read about services in my community.

☐ 3. Scan for specific information.

☐ 4. Understand the simple present tense.

☐ 5. Use a T-chart to organize information.

☐ 6. _____

Fun and Relaxation

In this unit, you will:

1. Read about exercise.
2. Read about lowering stress.
3. Use the context to figure out new words.
4. Understand adverbs of frequency.
5. Use a chart to compare information.

 Accessing Information

Talk About It

What are the people doing? Why? Are they having fun? Getting exercise? Relaxing?

You Decide

There are many ways to relax and have fun. What do you do for fun?

Key Vocabulary

A. In this unit, we will read about exercise and relaxation. Exercise is a good way to relax. First, work with a partner. What are some good ways to exercise? To relax? In your notebook, write a list.

B. Look at the pictures. Work with a partner. Take turns pointing at the words and saying them aloud.

exercise   **eat out**   **go to the movies**

EXERCISE 1   Fun Activities

A. What do your classmates like to do for fun? Ask 4 students. Complete the chart. Share your answers with the class. Use everyone's ideas to create a list of free time activities.

Name	Activity
Tim	swim

B. Look at the list you made in A. Are there any new activities you want to try? Tell the class.

Where can you find an inexpensive gym?

Community SPORTS Center

Are you tired?
Are you worried about your health?
Do you need more exercise?

JOIN the Community SPORTS Center

We offer:

A running track!

A swimming pool!

Indoor and outdoor basketball!

A weight room!

Baseball, basketball, football, and soccer teams for men and women!

The Community Sports Center is near offices and stores downtown.
Join NOW and get ready for summer!

Community SPORTS Center

1. The cost is $20 per month. You must pay by the first day of each month. You do not need to sign a contract.
2. You must bring your own towel.
3. We are closed on all major holidays.
4. Hours:
   Monday to Friday: 6:00 AM to 9:00 AM
       and 4:00 PM to 9:00 PM
   Saturday: 9:00 AM to 5:00 PM
   Sunday: 1:00 PM to 9:00 PM

EXERCISE 2   Yes or No

Write yes or **no** on the line.

_____ **1.** The ad is for the Community Sports Center.

_____ **2.** The Community Sports Center has a swimming pool.

_____ **3.** You can play baseball at the Community Sports Center.

_____ **4.** People can run at the Community Sports Center.

_____ **5.** The Community Sports Center is very expensive.

Enriching Your Vocabulary

There are many sports we can play. Look at the picture.

1. soccer 2. walking 3. weight lifting 4. running 5. swimming 6. tennis

EXERCISE 3   Equipment

What equipment do you need for each sport? Match. Find the
equipment in the picture.

_____b_____ **1.** running

_____ **2.** swimming

_____ **3.** soccer

_____ **4.** tennis

_____ **5.** weight lifting

a. tennis racket

b. good shoes

c. weights

d. ball

e. pool

Teamwork

Work with a partner. Student A looks at the Community Sports
Center information on page 84. Student B looks at the questions
on page 106. Answer Student B's questions. Then switch roles.
Are your answers the same?

Giving Voice

Talk It Over

A. John Turner is interested in getting more exercise. He lives far away from the Community Sports Center. But the Rooftop Club is near his apartment. So he got information about the Rooftop Club. Read the information. What do the clubs have? Fill in the chart. Write a check (√) in the chart.

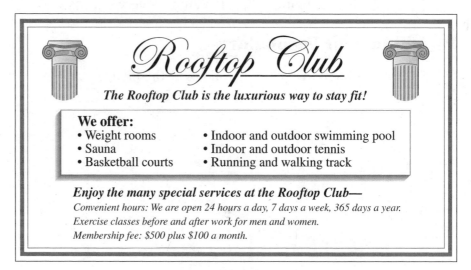

Rooftop Club

The Rooftop Club is the luxurious way to stay fit!

We offer:
- Weight rooms
- Sauna
- Basketball courts
- Indoor and outdoor swimming pool
- Indoor and outdoor tennis
- Running and walking track

Enjoy the many special services at the Rooftop Club—
Convenient hours: We are open 24 hours a day, 7 days a week, 365 days a year.
Exercise classes before and after work for men and women.
Membership fee: $500 plus $100 a month.

	Community Sports Center	Rooftop Club
Indoor pool	√	√
Basketball		
Tennis		
Exercise classes		
Inexpensive		

B. John doesn't have a lot of money. He wants to swim and play tennis. Which place should he join? Why? Talk over your ideas with a small group. Share your ideas with the class.

EXERCISE 4   You Decide

A. There are many reasons why we exercise. Why do you want to exercise? Circle. Then talk over your answer with a partner.

relax   have fun with friends   lose weight   improve my health

B. Where can you exercise in your community? With your partner, write a list in your notebooks. Which one do you want to use? Why? Tell the class.

park

Accessing Information

Talk About It

Community SPORTS Center

Adult Walking Club

Do you love to walk for fun?
Then **join** the Adult Walking Club at the **Community Sports Center.**
We walk at Lake Park every Saturday at 9:00 AM and every Sunday at 1:00 PM.

Meet new friends!   **Relax and enjoy beautiful Lake Park!**
Get exercise!   **Best of all, it's FREE!**

Work with a partner. What do the pictures and words tell you about the Community Sports Center walking club? What kind of people will want to join the club? Do you want to join the walking club? Why or why not?

READING STRATEGY
Use the Context to Figure Out New Words

When you read, you may see new words. When you see a new word, you can use the other words in the sentence to figure out the meaning. For example, look at this sentence: We ate some delicious **krittles** at the restaurant last night.

The word **krittle** is not really an English word. But you can figure out what it probably means from other words in the sentence: **delicious, ate, restaurant.** It must be a kind of food.

When you figure out meanings from context, you can read faster and better. The reading on the next page is about stress. What does **stress** mean? As you read, use the other words to figure out the meaning of **stress.**

What is STRESS?

How can you lower your stress?

Amalia Paz is a very busy person. She and her husband, Martin, have three children. The oldest child, Martin Jr., is in college. The other two children, Brian and Louisa, are in high school. Amalia is a teacher's aide at South Side High School. She is taking classes at a university, too.

Amalia Paz says, "Right now I am under a lot of stress. I never relax. I work because Martin's college bills are very expensive. I work every day from 8:00 to 3:00. I also have to go to meetings at school. Then I have class at the university from 5:00 to 9:00 Monday and Wednesday. Those classes are expensive, too. Brian and Louisa don't drive, so I usually have to take them to soccer, the library, and their friends' houses in my car. Every night I have to do my homework and get ready for work."

Is your life like Amalia's?

Take this quiz and find out. Circle YES or NO.

1. Do you get exercise 3 times a week?   YES   NO

2. Do you take time to relax every day?   YES   NO

3. Do you eat at home at least 5 times a week?   YES   NO

4. Do you sleep 8 hours every night?   YES   NO

How many times did you answer NO? If you answered NO 3–4 times, you need to reduce your stress. Here are some ideas.

1. You should exercise for an hour 3 times a week.

2. Take time to relax every day. Read a book, go to the movies, call a friend, or write a letter.

3. Get 8 hours of sleep every night.

4. Try to eat at home most of the time. Only eat out once in a while.

All of these ideas can lower your stress. Try one or two of them today!

EXERCISE 5 Meaning from Context

A. Work with a partner. What does **stress** mean? Write a few words in your notebook. What words in the article helped you figure out the meaning of stress? Tell the class.

B. Work with your partner. Find another word in the article that you do not understand. Use the other words to figure out the meaning. Share the word and the meaning with the class.

EXERCISE 6 Answer the Questions

1. Why is Amalia Paz under a lot of stress? _____

_____

2. What can Amalia do to lower her stress? Check the boxes.

   ☐ eat out on Saturday nights

   ☐ eat out every night

   ☐ go to the movies

   ☐ do extra work

   ☐ _____

LANGUAGE NOTE
Adverbs of Frequency

The reading on lowering stress uses adverbs of frequency. Adverbs of frequency tell how often we do something. Understanding adverbs of frequency will help you improve your reading skills.

Amalia **always** feels stressed.

She worries about her problems **every day**.

She **never** sleeps 8 hours a night.

Here are some common adverbs of frequency:

every day   once in a while   usually   never   once a day   5 times a week

Review the article. Circle the adverbs of frequency.

EXERCISE 7 Adverbs of Frequency

In your notebook, write a few sentences about your free time activities. Use adverbs of frequency. Then read your sentences to a partner. Share your partner's sentences with the class.

STUDY SKILL
Figuring Out New Words

When you read, you see new words. When you see a new word, there are several things you can do.

1. Skip the word. Read the sentence or the paragraph again. If you understand, then you do not need to know the new word.
2. Get the meaning from the context. Use the other words to figure out the new word.
3. Use a dictionary if you cannot figure out the new word.

When you learn a new word, write the word and its definition in your notebook.

too much work

☝ Taking Action

A. These days, everyone is under stress. Why are you under stress? Write a few words in your notebook. Share your ideas with your partner. Why is your partner under stress? Tell the class.

B. What can your partner do to relax?

🌉 Bridging to the Future

A. Mohamed Tahiri is under a lot of stress. He wants to lower his stress. He wrote these notes. Will these ideas help him lower his stress? Why? Tell a partner.

Strategy	Ideas
Exercise	Play soccer on Sunday. Lift weights on Tuesday and Thursday after work.
Take time to relax	Go to the movies with friends on Saturday night. Eat out with my friends on Sunday.
Sleep	Go to bed at 10:00. Get up at 6:00.

B. You want to lower your stress. In your notebook, make a chart about yourself. Follow the example in A. Then share your ideas with your partner.

⊂⊃ Workplace Connection

A. Many people get a lot of exercise at work. Cooks, nurses, and others walk a lot at work. But other workers, like taxi drivers and office workers, don't get a lot of exercise. How can these workers get more exercise at work? Work with a partner and make a list.

B. Sometimes we feel stressed at work. What can we do to lower our stress at work? For example, a customer upsets you. You want to yell at the customer. So quietly count to ten. Then you will be less stressed. Work with a partner. Think of ways that you can lower your stress at work. Share your ideas with the class.

Review

EXERCISE 8 Meaning from Context

Read about the museum. What does the word **exhibit** mean? Use the other words in the paragraph to figure it out. Write a definition in your notebook.

Science and Technology Museum

Special Exhibit   **CHOCOLATE!**

This special exhibit tells about the history of everyone's favorite food—chocolate. Find out how chocolate is made. See chocolate food and drinks from different countries around the world. Watch our cooks make chocolate treats right before your eyes! Try new chocolate treats in the chocolate gift shop and restaurant.

EXERCISE 9 Answer the Questions

Write your answers in your notebook.

1. Where is the exhibit?

2. What is the exhibit about?

3. Can seeing the exhibit help you lower your stress? Why do you think so?

Your Portfolio

In Bridging to the Future on page 90, you wrote about ways to lower your stress. Rewrite your ideas on a sheet of paper and put them in your portfolio.

Summing Up

I can:

☐ 1. Read about exercise.

☐ 2. Read about lowering stress.

☐ 3. Use the context to figure out new words.

☐ 4. Understand adverbs of frequency.

☐ 5. Use a chart to compare information.

☐ 6. _____

Lifelong Learning

In this unit, you will:

1. Read about computer training.
2. Read an article about education.
3. Read and make inferences.
4. Understand **should**.
5. Use charts to organize information.

 **Accessing Information**

Talk About It

What are the people doing? Where are they? What are they learning? Name other places people can learn.

You Decide

People agree that learning is important. Why is learning important to you?

Key Vocabulary

A. In this unit, you will read about school and computers. First, work with a partner. In your notebook, complete the chart. Write words related to school and computers. Follow the example.

School	Computers
teacher	*Internet*

B. Study the vocabulary.

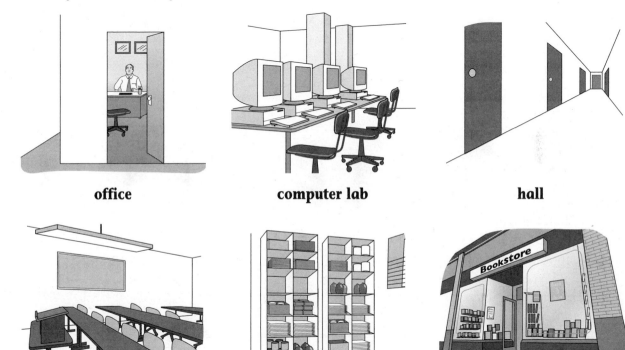

office   computer lab   hall

classroom   supply room   bookstore

EXERCISE 1   Places at School

You want to do these things. Where do you go? Write the place on the line.

1. It's time for your English class. _____

2. You need to send an e-mail. _____

3. Your teacher wants you to get some paper and chalk. _____

4. You want to buy a new dictionary. _____

5. You need to talk to the director of the school. _____

How do you send an e-mail?

Henry and Wan Chin want to get a computer. The computer store has inexpensive classes. Wan just took a class about e-mail. She got this information at the class.

TRACK 19

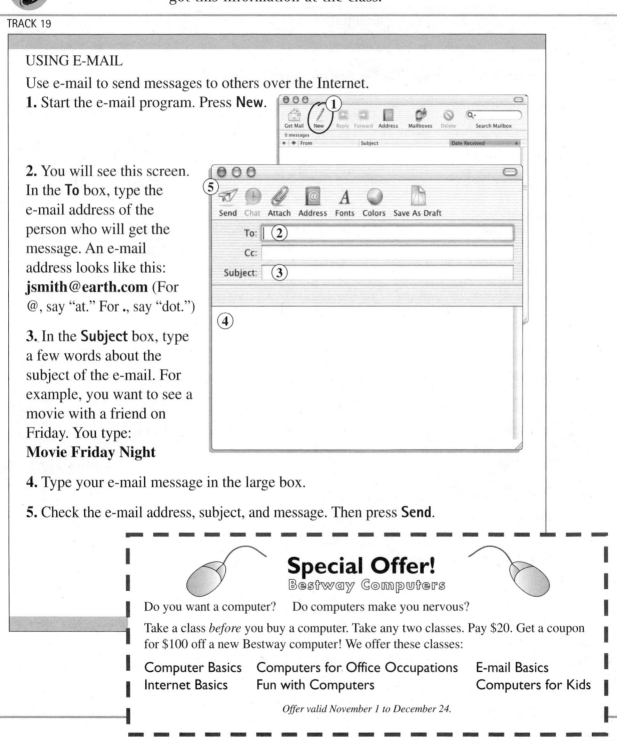

USING E-MAIL

Use e-mail to send messages to others over the Internet.

1. Start the e-mail program. Press **New**.

2. You will see this screen. In the **To** box, type the e-mail address of the person who will get the message. An e-mail address looks like this: **jsmith@earth.com** (For @, say "at." For ., say "dot.")

3. In the **Subject** box, type a few words about the subject of the e-mail. For example, you want to see a movie with a friend on Friday. You type: **Movie Friday Night**

4. Type your e-mail message in the large box.

5. Check the e-mail address, subject, and message. Then press **Send**.

EXERCISE 2 Yes or No

Write yes or **no** on the line.

_____ **1.** Wan and Henry took a class on e-mail.

_____ **2.** Bestway Computers has computer classes.

_____ **3.** You can learn to use computers in the classes.

_____ **4.** You can learn to make computers in the classes.

_____ **5.** People who take two classes get a coupon for a free computer.

EXERCISE 3 Sending an E-mail

Number the steps in order from 1 to 5.

_____ a. Type the subject of the e-mail.

_____ b. Press **Send.**

_____ c. Type the e-mail message.

_____ d. Type the e-mail address.

_____ e. Press **New.**

EXERCISE 4 Think About It

Circle the letter of the answer.

1. Why does Bestway Computers have classes?
   a. Bestway Computers makes a lot of money.
   b. People learn about computers. Then they buy computers.

2. The special offer is from November 1 to December 24. Many people buy and give gifts at this time of year. What does Bestway Computers want customers to do?
   a. Give classes to their families.
   b. Buy computers and give them to people.

Enriching Your Vocabulary

Study the vocabulary.

1. **keyboard** Use it to type information.
2. **screen** Use it to see information.
3. **printer** Use it to print information.
4. **mouse** Use it to point at information on the screen.

Teamwork

Work with a partner. Student A looks at the coupon on page 94. Student B looks at the questions on page 106. Answer Student B's questions. Then switch roles. Are your answers the same?

EXERCISE 5   Pick a Class

What class should the people take? Write the letter of the class on the line.

a. Computer Basics
b. Computers for Office Occupations
c. Fun with Computers
d. Computers for Kids

_____ **1.** Jorge doesn't know anything about computers.

_____ **2.** Patricia wants to watch movies on her new computer.

_____ **3.** Ahn is 11 years old. He wants to use computers at school.

_____ **4.** Lance is a file clerk. He wants to become an administrative assistant.

LANGUAGE NOTE
Should

We use **should** and **shouldn't** when we give advice.

You **should** learn to use computers.

You **shouldn't** buy an expensive computer right away.

How to do an Internet search

EXERCISE 6   Should

A. What do you want to learn about computers? Write a few ideas in your notebook.

B. Read your ideas to your partner. Which class should you take at Bestway Computers? Ask your partner. Which class should your partner take? Give advice. Use **should**. Share your answer with the class.

STUDY SKILL
Getting Access to a Computer

Not everyone can buy a computer. But there are many places to use a computer for free or at low cost. Try the computer lab at your school, the library, a copy shop, or an Internet café. There are also many free or inexpensive ways to use e-mail. Ask your teacher to help you find these resources.

Accessing Information

Talk About It

What information do these ads tell you? What information is not in the ads? Which of these ads interests you most? Why? Which ad does not interest you? Why not?

READING STRATEGY
Read and Make Inferences

When you make inferences, you use the information in a reading to figure out more information. You can use information in a reading to figure out many things. For example, you know Bestway Computers has computer classes. But why does the store have the classes? You figured out the answer: the store has classes so people will buy computers from the store.

Why did the school win an award?

COMMUNITY NEWS

Hillcrest Adult Learning Center Receives an Award

Hillcrest Adult Learning Center received an excellence award from the State Department of Education. **The award is $10,000.**

People at Hillcrest are happy about the award. Ms. Marilyn Barton, dean, said, "This award is for all of the learners and teachers at Hillcrest." Frank Rodriguez, president of the Student Association, said, "Our school is getting this award because of our excellent teachers and our wonderful students."

Hillcrest Adult Learning Center has 800 students. The school has English classes, cooking classes, and classes in child care, car repair, and heating and air conditioning. Adults can also finish high school at Hillcrest.

Plans for the Money

Dean Barton said that the school is making plans for the money. "Everyone has a different plan for the money, so we are going to have a school meeting to discuss the award. We will invite learners, teachers, and community leaders to the meeting."

We asked several people at Hillcrest for ideas about the award money.

Frank Rodriguez, President of the Student Association

Let's give each class some money. The class can use the money for books, a new computer, or other things that the students need.

Amanda Lo, Teacher

The supply room is empty. We need books. We need paper and a new copier. The school should get supplies for teachers.

Edna Appleby, Custodian

The school building needs a lot of repairs. The halls need new paint. We also need new furniture for the classrooms and offices. A lot of the desks are old and broken. Students need a bookstore, too. They can buy books and supplies there. A bookstore can sell drinks and snacks, too.

Roberta Olmos, Assistant Dean

Our school does not have computer classes. Our students need computer skills to get good jobs. We should use the money to start a computer lab.

EXERCISE 7   Answer the Questions

1. Why did Hillcrest win an award?

2. What was the award?

3. Does the school have a plan for the money?

4. How many people study at Hillcrest?

5. What do people study at Hillcrest?

6. What will the people talk about at the meeting?

EXERCISE 8   Making Inferences

Hillcrest Adult Learning Center won an award because it's a good school. What do you think makes this learning center good? Write a few ideas in your notebook. Share your ideas with the class.

EXERCISE 9   Organizing Information

A. What do people at Hillcrest want to do with the award money? Complete the chart.

Name	Role	Idea
Frank Rodriguez	President of Student Association	Give each class some money.
Amanda Lo		
Edna Appleby		
Roberta Olmos		

B. Look at the people's ideas. Do the people agree? Are their ideas related to their roles? Explain.

Talk It Over

Work in a group of three learners. One is a student, one is a teacher, and one is a school worker (custodian, librarian, etc.). Each person should make a plan for the money. Then talk over the plans. Try to figure out one plan for the money. Do you agree? Why or why not? Share your ideas with the class.

EXERCISE 10   Should

As you know, **should** is used to give advice. Review the reading. Circle the examples of **should**.

Taking Action

A. People want to learn many things. For example, John wants to learn to cook so he can become a cook in a restaurant. He also wants to learn to use a computer. Finally, he wants to learn to lift weights safely. He made this plan.

What I Want to Learn	Where I Will Learn It
cook	City Restaurant School
use a computer	class at computer store
lift weights	Community Sports Center

B. Complete the plan for yourself. Then share your plan with a partner. What does your partner want to learn? Tell the class.

What I Want to Learn	Where I Will Learn It

Bridging to the Future

Work with a small group. You want to make schools in your city better. What should the city do? Write a list of ideas in your notebook. Share your ideas with the class. Use everyone's ideas to create a class list.

Workplace Connection

Companies often offer training to workers. What training should companies offer their workers? Work with a small group. Write a list in your notebooks. Share your ideas with the class. Use everyone's ideas to create a class list.

Review

EXERCISE 11   Inferences

Fatima Benali is a student at Hillcrest Adult Learning Center. Read her idea about spending the award money. Then answer the questions.

> Students worked really hard to win this award, so I think that we should spend the money to help the students. The biggest problem for a lot of students is child care. Students can't come to school because they don't have child care. We should use the money to start a child care center.

1. Fatima wants to use the money to help students
   a. with high test scores.
   b. with children.
   c. who don't have cars.

2. Fatima is probably interested in child care because
   a. she doesn't like children.
   b. she has children.
   c. she is a good student.

EXERCISE 12   Should

Your teacher has $100 to spend on supplies. What should she do with the money? In your notebook, write 3 sentences with **should**.

Your Portfolio

In Taking Action on page 100, you wrote a plan for what you want to learn. Put a copy of your plan in your portfolio.

Summing Up

I can:

☐ 1. Read about computer training.

☐ 2. Read an article about education.

☐ 3. Read and make inferences.

☐ 4. Understand **should**.

☐ 5. Use charts to organize information.

☐ 6. _____

Teamwork

For each Teamwork activity, Student A follows the instructions on the Student Book page. Student B follows the instructions here.

Unit 1, Page 5

Work with a partner. Student A looks at the class schedule on page 4. Student B looks at his or her schedule on this page. When can you study English? Ask Student A. Then switch roles and repeat the activity.

My Schedule

Activity	Time & Location	
Work	Monday to Friday	7:00 AM to 3:00 PM
Food Service Class	Monday & Wednesday	5:00 PM to 8:00 PM

Unit 2, Page 15

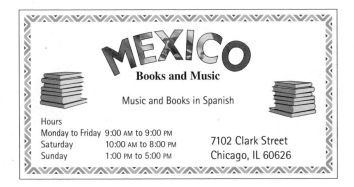

MEXICO

Books and Music

Music and Books in Spanish

Hours
Monday to Friday 9:00 AM to 9:00 PM
Saturday   10:00 AM to 8:00 PM
Sunday   1:00 PM to 5:00 PM

7102 Clark Street
Chicago, IL 60626

Work with a partner. Student A looks at the business card on page 14. Student B looks at the business card on this page. Ask questions about Student A's business card and complete the chart. Answer Student A's questions about your business card. Then switch roles and repeat the activity.

What's the name of the business?	
What city is it in?	
What does it sell?	
Does it sell magazines?	
Is it open on Sunday?	

Unit 3, Page 25

Work with a partner. Student A looks at Kathy Ross's time card on page 24. Student B looks at Frank Stover's time card on this page. Ask Student A the questions about Kathy Ross. Write the answers in your notebook. Answer Student A's questions about Frank Stover. Then switch roles and repeat the activity.

1. What time does Kathy usually start work?

2. Was Kathy late to work this week? What day?

3. Was Kathy absent this week?

4. Did Kathy work late this week?

5. Should Kathy get the bonus this week? Why or why not?

Name:		Frank Stover
IN	Monday	5:00 AM
OUT		12:00 PM
IN	Tuesday	5:00 AM
OUT		12:00 PM
IN	Wednesday	5:00 AM
OUT		12:00 PM
IN	Thursday	5:00 AM
OUT		1:00 PM
IN	Friday	Vacation Day
OUT		Vacation Day

Unit 4, Page 35

Work with a partner. Student A looks at the Greatway ad on page 34. Student B looks at the Food Town ad on this page. Complete the chart. Ask Student A about the prices at Greatway. If a food item is not on sale, write **Not on sale.** Then look at the information. Where do you want to shop? Discuss with your partner. Then share your answers with the class.

Food	Sale Price at Greatway	Sale Price at Food Town
Tomatoes	$.99	$1.19
Grapes		
Bananas		
Lettuce		

Food Town

Bananas
Sale price
39¢ a pound
Regular price $.69 a pound

Tomatoes
Sale price
1 19 a pound
Regular price $1.89 a pound

Lettuce
Sale price
25¢
Regular price $1.99

Unit 5, Page 45

Work with a partner. Student A looks at the safety instructions on page 44. Student B looks at the questions on this page. Ask Student A the questions. Write the answers in your notebook. Then switch roles and repeat the activity. Are your answers the same?

1. I have a bad cold. I feel terrible, and I'm very tired. Should I go to work today? Why?

2. I work in a parking garage. I park people's cars. Sometimes people are in a hurry. They want me to run to get their cars. Is that a good idea? Why?

3. I think that the brakes on my delivery truck are not working properly. What should I do? Why?

4. My company put up a new safety sign. I don't understand all the words. What should I do? Why?

Unit 6, Page 55

Work with a partner. Student A looks at the rates and services on page 54. Student B looks at the questions on this page. Ask Student A the questions. Write the answers in your notebook.

1. Marta wants voice mail and voice dialing. How much will she pay a month?

2. Paul wants caller ID and a second phone line for his computer. How much will he pay a month?

3. Tim wants call forwarding and voice mail. How much will he pay a month?

Now switch roles and repeat the activity. Are your answers the same?

Unit 7, Page 65

Work with a partner. Student A looks at the museum information on page 64. Student B looks at the questions on this page. Ask Student A the questions. Write the answers in your notebook. Then switch roles. Are your answers the same?

1. What countries are the museums about?

2. What city are the museums in?

3. Can you find out about Mexican scientists at the museums?

4. Which museum probably has information about Chopin?

5. Do the museums have Web sites?

Unit 8, Page 75

Work with a partner. Student A looks at the apartment ad on page 74. Student B looks at the questions on this page. Ask Student A the questions. Write the answers in your notebook. Then switch roles. Compare your answers.

1. How much is the rent?

2. How much is the deposit?

3. How many bedrooms does the apartment have?

4. How many bathrooms does the apartment have?

5. What number do people call for information?

Unit 9, Page 85

Work with a partner. Student A looks at the Community Sports Center information on page 84. Student B looks at the questions on this page. Ask Student A the questions. Write the answers in your notebook. Then switch roles. Are your answers the same?

1. How much does the sports center cost per month?

2. Do you need to bring a towel?

3. Can you use the sports center on Sunday?

4. Can you go to the sports center at 6:00 on Monday morning?

5. Can you use the sports center on New Year's Day?

Unit 10, Page 95

Work with a partner. Student A looks at the coupon on page 94. Student B looks at the questions on this page. Ask Student A the questions. Write the answers in your notebook. Then switch roles. Are your answers the same?

1. Can you study computer basics at Bestway Computers?

2. You took one class. Can you get a $100 coupon?

3. How many classes do you have to take to get a $100 coupon?

4. How much do two classes cost?

5. Matilda took two computer classes and got a coupon. She used the coupon to get a new computer. How much money did she save?

Learning Journal

Make a photocopy of this page after you complete each unit.

In the first column, write what you learned in the unit. Look at the Summing Up section on the last page of each unit for ideas. Then add other things you learned.

In the second column, write what you want to learn in the future.

In Unit _____, I learned . . .	I still want to learn . . .

Vocabulary Index

I

immigrant (Unit 7, 63)
instructions (Unit 6, 58)
insurance (Unit 2, 15)
injured (Unit 5, 43)

J

January (Unit 3, 23)
July (Unit 3, 23)
June (Unit 3, 23)

K

keyboard (Unit 10, 95)
keyboarding (Unit 1, 3)

L

lawyer (Unit 7, 68)
lettuce (Unit 4, 34)
library (Unit 8, 73)

M

machines (Unit 5, 44)
mail carrier (Unit 2, 13)
mall (Unit 8, 73)
March (Unit 3, 23)
math (Unit 1, 3)
May (Unit 3, 23)
mayor (Unit 7, 68)
message (Unit 6, 53)
metalworking (Unit 1, 3)
miss (a call) (Unit 6, 53)
Monday (Unit 3, 23)
mother (Unit 2, 13)
mouse (Unit 10, 95)
movies (Unit 9, 83)
mural (Unit 7, 63)
musician (Unit 7, 63)

N

neighborhood (Unit 8, 73)
noodles (Unit 4, 33)
November (Unit 3, 23)

O

October (Unit 3, 23)
office skills (Unit 1, 3)
office (Unit 10, 93)
onions (Unit 4, 41)
organization (Unit 7, 68)

P

park (Unit 8, 73)
permission (Unit 2, 17)
plug in (Unit 6, 53)
poison (Unit 5, 43)
police officer (Unit 2, 13)
politician (Unit 7, 63)
post office (Unit 8, 73)
potatoes (Unit 4, 36)
pound (Unit 4, 33)
press (Unit 6, 53)
prices (Unit 4, 34)
printer (Unit 10, 95)

R

reading (Unit 1, 3)
rent (Unit 8, 74)
ring (Unit 6, 53)
rules (Unit 5, 43)
run (Unit 5, 43)
running track (Unit 9, 84)
running (Unit 9, 85)

S

safety glasses (Unit 5, 43)
safety gloves (Unit 5, 43)
safety shoes sale (Unit 4, 34)
sale (Unit 4, 34)
Saturday (Unit 3, 23)
school (Unit 8, 73)
screen (Unit 10, 95)
September (Unit 3, 23)
services (Unit 8, 73)
sign (Unit 5, 43)

sister (Unit 2, 13)
sleeping (Unit 1, 3)
slip (Unit 5, 43)
smoke alarm (Unit 2, 18)
soccer (Unit 9, 84)
son (Unit 2, 13)
spaghetti (Unit 4, 33)
Spanish (Unit 1, 3)
start (Unit 6, 53)
stop (Unit 6, 53)
students (Unit 1, 4)
Sunday (Unit 3, 23)
supermarket (Unit 8, 73)
supply room (Unit 10, 93)
swimming pool (Unit 9, 84)
swimming (Unit 9, 85)

T
tennis (Unit 9, 85)
Thursday (Unit 3, 23)
tomatoes (Unit 4, 34)
Tuesday (Unit 3, 23)
type (Unit 10, 94)

U
union (Unit 7, 68)

V
vote (Unit 7, 68)

W
walking (Unit 1, 3)
walking (Unit 9, 85)
Wednesday (Unit 3, 23)
weight lifting (Unit 9, 85)
weight room (Unit 9, 84)
wife (Unit 2, 13)

Skills Index